PENGUIN

SELECTIONS FROM THE *CARMINA BURANA*

ADVISORY EDITOR: BETTY RADICE

David Parlett was born in London in 1939, educated at Battersea Grammar School and took his degree in Modern Languages at the University College of Wales, Aberystwyth. He was a teacher, a technical journalist and then in public relations before establishing himself as a freelance author and games-inventor. In this capacity he is an acknowledged expert on the history of card games and the author of three Penguin originals: *Card Games*, *Patience* and *Word Games*.

His interest in translating the *Carmina Burana* is of many years' standing and results inevitably from a conjunction of interests in history, poetry and linguistics. Even the games interest is relevant, he asserts, pointing to the example of J. D. Huizinga, whose *Homo Ludens* and *The Waning of the Middle Ages* are classics in their respective fields.

David Parlett is married and lives in South London with his wife and two children.

David Parlett

SELECTIONS FROM THE

CARMINA BURANA

*

A VERSE TRANSLATION

Penguin Books

PENGUIN BOOKS

Published by the Penguin Group
Penguin Books Ltd, 80 Strand, London WC2R 0RL, England
Penguin Group (USA) Inc., 375 Hudson Street, New York, New York 10014, USA
Penguin Group (Canada), 90 Eglinton Avenue East, Suite 700, Toronto, Ontario, Canada M4P 2Y3
(a division of Pearson Penguin Canada Inc.)
Penguin Ireland, 25 St Stephen's Green, Dublin 2, Ireland
(a division of Penguin Books Ltd)
Penguin Group (Australia), 250 Camberwell Road,
Camberwell, Victoria 3124, Australia (a division of Pearson Australia Group Pty Ltd)
Penguin Books India Pvt Ltd, 11 Community Centre,
Panchsheel Park, New Delhi – 110 017, India
Penguin Group (NZ), cnr Airborne and Rosedale Roads, Albany,
Auckland 1310, New Zealand (a division of Pearson New Zealand Ltd)
Penguin Books (South Africa) (Pty) Ltd, 24 Sturdee Avenue,
Rosebank, Johannesburg 2196, South Africa

Penguin Books Ltd, Registered Offices: 80 Strand, London WC2R 0RL, England

First published 1986
015

Printed and bound in Great Britain
by Clays Ltd, Elcograf S.p.A.
Filmset in 10/13pt Linotron Sabon by
Rowland Phototypesetting Ltd,
Bury St Edmunds, Suffolk

ISBN: 978-0-14-044440-7

www.greenpenguin.co.uk

To Norah Granger

Gaude quod primam   te sors mihi fecit amicam

CONTENTS

CONTENTS

INTRODUCTION

Outside a specialized readership *Carmina Burana* is probably best known as the title of a popular work for chorus and orchestra by Carl Orff. The hour-long cantata, much performed and recorded, is an exuberant setting of some twenty poems in Medieval Latin and Middle High German from a thirteenth-century manuscript found at Benediktbeuern in Bavaria (whence the title, 'Songs of Beuern'). They are essentially secular pieces, of varying degrees of literary merit, and covering a range of themes including satire, literary and liturgical parody, love songs, drinking songs and stories from the classics. As the largest – and most varied – surviving anthology of Medieval Latin poetry, the manuscript represents the last outpourings of poets who still used the language as fluently as their native tongues.

The present selection originated in a desire to provide an intelligible English text to the cantata: one that would follow the same metrical and rhyming patterns as the Latin, and so be singable to Orff's tunes. The result proved too short for independent publication, and I was invited to essay a larger collection drawn from the whole manuscript. This proved a welcome, if daunting, invitation; for although the popularity of the music at least puts the text into the public consciousness, the cantata's comparative brevity and contrived dramatic form tend to obscure the size, nature and importance of its literary source. Carl Orff necessarily restricted himself to about twenty pieces from a total of some 350 (depending on how they are counted). Many of his settings are of selected extracts from longer poems whose tenor, when considered as a whole, does not always accord with those portions emanating from the concert hall. If we add that he worked from editions of the text which have since been corrected in many important respects (and take into account various other criticisms of an extra-musical nature) it becomes understandable why Orff has not endeared himself to latter-day medieval scholars, who tend to regard the text not just as sacrosanct but as private property to boot.

Apart from a manuscript facsimile, the *Carmina Burana* has never been published as a whole in an English edition, and such parts of it as have already been 'done into English' – to borrow Omar/Fitzgerald's felicitous phrase – are scattered through various publications not now easy to come by. In making my selection, which in terms of linage represents about 20–25 per cent of the whole, I have been guided by two complementary and sometimes conflicting considerations. One was a desire to reflect the variety of the original collection by covering as many different genres and subjects as possible, even if some are of little intrinsic literary merit or seem out of joint with modern preoccupations. The other was a need to concentrate on those pieces most amenable to a fairly literal line-by-line treatment in English verse without having to wander too far from the poet's chosen form, or from my understanding of his intentions. Compromise has been inevitable. In some cases I have attempted the impossible for the sake of being representative; in others I have rejected the intractable for fear of being inaccurate.

I also wished to cater both for those whose only knowledge of the *Carmina Burana* is the cantata by Orff and for those who feel that his idiosyncratic concert selection does the original a disservice. I have therefore included in their entirety all the pieces which the composer used either wholly or in part, and gathered together in an appendix an English-language version of the concert selection so that it may be followed separately if required.

Language

Although none is named in the manuscript, some of the authors have been identified through other sources. They prove to have been of various nationalities, and hence native speakers of various tongues including English, French, German and other vernaculars of the time. They wrote in Latin because at the time of composition literacy was synonymous with Latinity. To read and write was by definition to read and write Latin – and to speak it, think in it, perchance to dream in it as well. It was the international language of western Europe and the Church – or of Christendom, to combine two modern concepts in one medieval term. Learning was traditionally a function of the religious life, and such education as there was lay in the hands of the Church and the monasteries. The first step in education was necessarily the acquisition of Latin, since it was the everyday medium of instruction for everything that followed.

As a spoken language, Medieval Latin differed significantly from the over-refined medium of the classical authors, from which it does not stand in true line of descent. Though a subtle and versatile literary vehicle in its own right, it may be traced back rather to the everyday spoken language of the Roman people ('Vulgar Latin') as employed by early Christian users, who found themselves unable to spread the word if the word was one which only the educated classes could understand. Medieval Latin is essentially Christian Latin – the tongue of men and angels, as opposed to that of decadent emperors and pagan gods. ('A man who is asking God to forgive his sins,' said St Augustine, 'does not much care whether the third syllable of *ignoscere* is pronounced long or short.') By comparison with Classical Latin, its counterpart, the language may be described as rationalized, practical and commonsensical. Characteristic features include a preference for short sentences with few subordinate clauses, a tendency to analytic rather than synthetic modes of expression, a shift to logical rather than emotional word order, the reduction of declensions and conjugations, and many phonetic simplifications, including loss of common diphthongs.

At the time of the *carmina Burana*, however, Latin was being challenged as a literary medium by such current vernacular languages as French (including Anglo-Norman), German and

Provençal, which had hitherto been the vehicles of a largely oral tradition. These and other evolving national languages were becoming a normal means of self-expression in the written as well as the spoken word. Fluency in Latin did not die overnight, but thereafter, outside the religious life, the language tended to restrict itself to the comparatively impersonal contexts of law, science and administration. The challenge of the vernaculars is hinted at in the *carmina* themselves, which include a large number of folk songs, dance songs and scholars' lyrics in Middle High German. The proportion of these that is unique to the Buranian manuscript is even higher than that of the Latin, and hence is of inestimable value to the history of German literature.

Background

The *carmina Burana* are of particular historical interest for the period they reflect, for although the manuscript dates from the thirteenth century, most of its contents were written in the twelfth, during the reigns of Louis VII and Philippe Auguste of France, Henry II of England and his wife Eleanor of Aquitaine, and Friedrich Barbarossa of Germany. Hence they are products of a cultural period which is now looked upon as a renaissance – one that antedates the *quattrocento* by three hundred years and centres on Paris rather than Florence, but may, perhaps, be regarded as an overture to that which is normally spelt with a capital 'R'.

The twelfth century was a period of comparative peace and prosperity. European invasions were long over, and successive popes had used crusades as an effective way of diverting society's bellicose elements from Christendom (Europe) to Palestine (the Middle East) in quest of fame and fortune – or, if the worst came to the worst, guaranteed salvation. Populations grew, and with them the technology required for more efficient food production. Agricultural techniques improved: the cheap but lumbering ox was replaced by the dearer but more cost-effective horse; watermills gave people new ideas about energy, leading to what has been termed the twelfth-century industrial revolution (Gimpel, *The Medieval Machine*). The newfangled European windmill, which was vertical as opposed to oriental-horizontal, appeared by the end of the century. The philosophers' stone, prime goal of previous scientific endeavour, would soon be replaced by the more rational, if equally impossible, quest for perpetual motion.

New land was being reclaimed from the sea, marshes were drained and forests cleared – as much for timber as for land. Canals were dug, and roads improved; towns revived, and new ones were built. Trade flourished; money again began to vie with property as the measure of private wealth; and avarice, a long-neglected member of the Seven Deadly Sins, enjoyed a popular comeback. Wealth, technology and piety combined to transform Romanesque into Gothic architecture, with its impossible combination of stone and mechanics to express space, light and timelessness.

The feudal class-system of priest, knight and peasant became complicated by a growth in occupational variety, by the absence of prominent people away on crusading business, by the beginnings of the bourgeoisie, by the increasingly necessary spread of educated people (clerks) through areas of society other than the purely religious. The first universities were founded, growing out of cathedral rather than monastery schools, and centring not on buildings but on famous teachers and their individual followings.

Add to the technological background a revival of learning, a rediscovery of the Latin classics and a new discovery of Greek and Arabic philosophical writings, and the inevitable result is a conflict between faith and reason. Such students as might 'eagerly frequent doctor and saint, and hear great argument about it and about' would find the conflict nowhere more dramatically embodied than in the long-running feud between Europe's leading intellectual, Peter Abélard (doctor), and most influential mystic, Bernard of Clairvaux (saint, eventually). 'By doubting,' asserted the one, 'we are led to questions; by questioning we arrive at the truth.' 'He deems himself by human reason to comprehend God altogether,' countered the other; 'he sees nothing as an enigma, nothing as in a glass darkly, but looks on everything face to face.' St Bernard twice had Abélard convicted of heretical teaching and forbidden to practise. The result was counterproductive, adding to Abélard's international fame and historical reputation (and leading soon to the institution of the Inquisition). Yet neither can be said to have won, for faith did not destroy reason nor reason faith – not even that of the devout Abélard. University education grew 'rational' to the point of sterility in the thirteenth century, by which time the founding of mendicant orders inspired by St Francis of Assisi had witnessed an ascent to new heights of practical faith. So students 'evermore came out by the same door as in they went'.

If Abélard is described as 'Europe's first intellectual' as a result of his conflict with St Bernard, he is also remembered as one of its most tragic lovers by association with Héloïse, and so introduces another significant facet of twelfth-century society – the role of women and the so-called discovery of romantic love.

Women were not admitted to the new-found universities, but this did not prevent their receiving education either privately or in religious houses – nunneries, convents, abbeys, priories, those traditional repositories of learning. Nor (as now) could they take holy orders, but neither did this prevent them from rising in the hierarchy of religious and educational life through those same institutions. Héloïse may have had Hebrew and Greek as well as Latin by the time she married Abélard at the age of seventeen. Within a few years of their physical separation and her taking of vows she was a prioress, and soon after became abbess of the Paraclete, a convent founded by Abélard. As abbess she exerted authority over associated monks and lay monks, and under her capable direction it became a model of Benedictine rule for women, giving rise to half a dozen daughter-houses.

Other notable women of the century ranged from the mystical Hildegard of Bingen (later canonized) to the political Eleanor of Aquitaine, Queen first of France and then of England (later idolized). Women wrote books, ran businesses, owned property and could be entitled to homage in their own right. 'They are to be seen buying, selling, effecting contracts, managing estates, and, at the end, making wills with a degree of liberty denied their sisters of the 16th to the 19th centuries' (Régine Pernoud, *La Femme au Temps des Cathédrales*).

A shift in the attitude of men to women, who were hitherto categorized as either simpering virgins or painted harlots, is marked at the start of the twelfth century by the unheralded accomplishment of troubadour literature. To oversimplify, the poetic muse forsook long, dreary epics about war and settled instead on short, sparkling lyrics about love. She was nurtured in the leisurely courts of Provence, where wealth encouraged the natural propensity of women to civilize society. Eleanor of Aquitaine herself was a product of the court of Poitiers, granddaughter of that same Guilhem IX who is credited as the first of the troubadours. What they created was not called 'courtly love' until the nineteenth century – to them it was *fin' amors*, or *honeste amare*, which today we might call 'true' or 'romantic' love: but they certainly created something novel, whose ideals gradually permeated all levels of twelfth-century society and have continued to colour western culture ever since.

There is argument as to the origins and definition of courtly love, not to mention its historical reality; but certain of its features are unmistakable, and are unmistakably set forth in the late-twelfth-century treatise *De Arte Honeste Amandi* by one Andreas Capellanus – Andrew the Chaplain (otherwise anonymous). In essence, women are exalted as the fount of all virtue: to love them is to worship them, to offer fealty to them and become their vassal – in theory not more than one at a time, as in the real feudal world. They are to be adored without hope of physical reward (*solacium*, 'solace'), but may be courted in accordance with strict rules of procedure partly dictated by their relative social standing. No woman is obliged to yield, or even expected to; but she is required to observe the proprieties, to assess and respect the worthiness of the suitor – in short, to recognize the rules of the game. If she does yield, it is out of 'generosity'. This gives rise to paradox, for consummation is regarded as virtually sacramental, yet 'pure love' – unplatonic to the point of naked embrace (but no further) – is, by the true believer, even more devoutly to be wished.

So man is ennobled by woman through love, whether requited or not. The ideal finds further expression in the development of that curious amalgam of love, piety and prowess called 'chivalry', which could not possibly have been invented in any other century. It also sees the gradual transformation of male-dominated epic literature into romance: the *Song of Roland* dates from the beginning of the twelfth century, the chivalry-centred Arthurian romances of Chrétien de Troyes from its last third. Which returns us again to the challenge of the vernaculars, for in so lively a century more people expect to be entertained in a language they can understand rather than in the Latin of the scholars. Women not only demanded vernacular literature but also wrote it: female troubadours included Beatritz of Dia, Marie de Champagne (the daughter of Eleanor of Aquitaine), and Marie de France (of unknown provenance).

The lyric poetry of the *carmina Burana* may be seen as a response to the spirit of the times by virtue of its secularity as well as its lyricism. It may represent the response of only one sex and one social stratum, and leave untouched many aspects of their physical world that we should wish to read about. Yet, to the extent that contemporary beliefs and preoccupations contribute to their inspiration, so the songs may contribute to our understanding of twelfth-century society, and thence, even, to our understanding of ourselves. For as F. B. Artz observes in *The Mind of the Middle Ages*, 'The development of culture in Latin Christendom was so remarkable in the twelfth and thirteenth centuries that they, rather than the fifteenth century, seem to represent the beginning of modern civilization.'

In any case, the Songs of Beuern are more than a cultural curiosity, more than sweepings from the floor of a proto-renaissance workshop. They are also both gripping and entertaining in their own right. Their composers are witty, urbane and charming, with no illusions about their own or their contemporaries' spiritual strengths and fleshly frailties, who find no subject too high or too low for their probing consideration and verbal dexterity. They write satires and panegyrics, hymns and pastorals, debates and monologues, crusading songs, begging songs, love songs, drinking songs, gaming songs, eating songs and songs of ineffable silliness. Literary merit is no *sine qua non* for inclusion in the anthology. 'Garlic and sapphires' are in its mud. There are gems of rare and luminous beauty: shining images like Diana's lantern in CB62, glimpses of ecstasy beyond the erotic, as in *Si linguis angelicis*, and passages of ingenious verbal dexterity (*Manus ferens munera*) in the cause of satire. Mingled amongst them are such cloves as a versified list of all known animals and the noises they make, a couplet of gobbledegook acting as a charm or incantation, and a dance song whose philosophical import is equivalent to that of the hokey-cokey. Some of the pieces sound like advertising jingles. Perhaps they are. They may be motivated by moral rather than commercial considerations, but the pressure they exert – that of social conformity – might appear, *mutatis mutandis*, much the same.

Title

Carmina Burana is the title given to the anthology by its first modern editor, Johann Schmeller, whose reading of the text was first published in 1847.

Carmina usually translates as 'songs' or 'poems' according to context. Confronted with printed verses today, we tend to expect poems rather than songs. The difference is more than musical. Songs are normally intended for public performance, but poems are more usually read silently and so felt to represent a private form of communication between poet and reader – a fact which enables, even encourages, them to be conceptually more complex and verbally more involved.

On the whole, the *carmina Burana* should be approached not just as poems but as lyrics – that is, poems intended to be sung.

This is emphasized by the fact that many of them are provided, in manuscript, with an indication of their accompanying tunes by means of staffless neumes. It seems likely that the compilers intended to do this for all the contents, though they did not complete the task. Neumes lack the precision of modern notation and give only an outline of an appropriate tune. This would not have worried the performers unduly. There were no demarcation disputes between writers, composers and performers: the most versatile lyricists were all three, and might equally be expected to write new melodies for existing words or new words for existing tunes, or to compose and perform new songs *ab initio*. Professional performers who were not necessarily composers – in court circles the *jongleurs* or, later, *ministeriales* (minstrels) – would know a stock of tunes and usually be able to find one to suit a given metrical format. (Church organists today have much the same ability.) Despite this imprecision, a number of tunes have been reconstructed from other sources, and recordings are now available of some of the *carmina Burana* as they might originally have been heard.

The fact that they are primarily songs is more obvious in some cases than in others. Some are deliberate nonsense songs; many are dance songs requiring no depth of thought or introspection to be expressed in the accompanying words. This is not to deny that many of the verses can indeed be read silently and responded to as personal communications between poet and reader. The ability to read silently to oneself (and without moving the lips – an accomplishment of St Jerome's which is reported to have so impressed his fourth-century admirers) was undoubtedly growing at this time, especially with the rise of universities, and must often have affected the poet's approach to his subject. The timeless nature of the text may reside in the fact that so many pieces are capable of being read in this way without jarring on the sensibilities.

Burana commemorates the place where the manuscript was found – or, to be precise, from which it had last come when its significance was initially appreciated. The town, now known as Benediktbeuern, lies in a valley of the Loisach a few kilometres north of the Kochelsee in the Upper Bavarian Alps between Munich and Innsbruck. Its monastery is the oldest in Bavaria, founded by St Boniface in 730–40 at a site then known simply as Buren (a common place-name element meaning 'houses' or 'buildings'). The chief relics of St Benedict were housed there for a while, until Charlemagne saw fit to distribute them more equitably throughout the German-speaking world. By the time the *carmina* were written the saint's name had attached itself to the town, which is recorded as *Benedictoburanum*.

To his title, 'The Songs of Beuern', Schmeller added the explanatory subtitle, 'Latin and German Songs and Poems from a Manuscript of the XIII Century emanating from Benedictbeuern [and held] at the Royal Library, Munich'. The words are carefully chosen, besides drawing attention to the 'songs and poems' aspect. The manuscript itself was compiled in the thirteenth century, but most of its contents have since been shown to date from the twelfth, while some additions are as late as the fourteenth. More importantly, the fact that the manuscript was found at Beuern does not necessarily mean that it originated there. None of the contents is demonstrably 'Buranian' by origin or reference; and the songs are not all of German authorship. Nor are they all unique to the Buranian text, for although it contains many medieval Latin lyrics not found elsewhere, a large proportion is well known from other manuscripts – in some cases better known and better transmitted. The 'Archpoet's Confession', for example, is recorded more or less complete in over thirty extant manuscripts of the time, with excerpts, extracts, accretions and parodies in many more.

For these reasons, the popular title is often eschewed in favour of the manuscript designation *Codex Buranus*.

Manuscript

Such of the Codex as survives consists mainly of 112 vellum folios bound in leather and housed at the Bayerische Staatsbibliothek in

Munich. It is neither complete nor bound in the original order of compilation. The library also houses a further seven folios, referred to as the *Fragmenta Burana*, which are shown to have formed part of the manuscript before binding took place: six of them lie properly between ff. 106 and 107, the seventh following f. 112, so that the whole of the extant manuscript consists of 119 folios or 238 'pages' of text.

The volume is surprisingly small, at first sight, for the amount of material contained: the twenty-two lines of writing on each page occupy an area of 11×18.2 cm, which is almost exactly the format of the one-volume paperback edition currently available in Germany. Compression is accounted for by the fact that vellum was always too precious to squander on the white space nowadays indulged in by typographical designers and concrete poets. The scribes in this case have followed customary medieval practice by using standard abbreviations and by writing verse as if it were prose. Only for the start of a new piece has a new line been embarked upon. Distinctions between lines of verse, stanzas and sections are drawn by means of a hierarchy of initial-letter treatments involving large capitals, small capitals and uncials.

The early Gothic script and late Romanesque style of the handful of illustrations date the manuscript to the first half of the thirteenth century, and internal evidence narrows this down to the years immediately preceding 1230 – except for the last remaining section (107 ff.), which seems to have been added between 1230 and 1250. It is chiefly the work of two scribes, designated h^1 and h^2, with a short section by a third hand hardly distinguishable from h^1 and so designated h^{1a}. Apparently h^1 was the senior partner of the undertaking: his collaborators were certainly more prone to misreadings and slips of the pen, and whereas h^1 has made corrections to all three hands – in some cases having erased and rewritten an entire piece by h^2 – there is no instance of corrections to h^1 by either of his colleagues.

One would like to know who initiated the undertaking. Was it h^1 himself, or should the work be regarded as a communal venture or a commission? Probably the latter. In his introduction to a facsimile edition of the text, Bernhard Bischoff summarizes the origin of the text as follows:

Around 1230 the manuscript was written in a southern border region of the Bavarian-speaking area, not far from Italian influence, perhaps in Carinthia, perhaps in Tyrol. Not long afterwards it was connected with a milieu through which the Marner had passed, and the latter's poem for the provost of Maria Saal would perhaps fix Carinthia as the area of origin. Since the codex seems to have been in the hands of students very soon thereafter and since a monastic environment seems improbable because of the script, one would think that the manuscript was compiled at the court of a prelate who was a lover of fine books and a patron of students.

Of the coloured miniatures, that of Dame Fortune controlling her wheel is particularly striking, and consequently the best known and most often reproduced (see cover illustration). It so struck the anonymous binder of the manuscript that he placed that section first in the book, so that she immediately greets the eye of the opener, though the associated songs (*Fortune plango vulnera* and *O Fortuna*) are now numbered 16 and 17 in the reconstituted order of composition. The section on love and spring includes two 'countryside in springtime' scenes and a love-couple illustrating *Suscipe, Flos, florem*. The drinking and gaming section has one drinking and three gaming scenes, the latter illustrating respectively dice, backgammon and chess. Two pen-and-ink line drawings have been added to margins at a later date: one shows a hand raised in blessing, the other, dating from about 1300 and associated with the love-debate between Phyllis and Flora, depicts a female figure presumably intended as Venus (though well wrapped up).

The history of the manuscript from 1250 onwards is obscure, except as may be deduced from the obvious ravages of time, use and abuse. Further entries were added by over thirty different hands, mostly in the last gathering (ff. 107–12) and in the *Fragmenta*, but also in margins and spaces of the original text. It seems that the last entries, generally more religious and pious in nature, were made neither with sympathy for nor with understanding of

the original compilers' intentions. Several correctors were sub-
sequently responsible for adding glosses, ascriptions, corrections
and hypercorrections. The last interpolations, dating from the
early fourteenth century, are the beginning of St John's Gospel in
German and a prayer to St Erasmus – the latter in a space made by
erasing a love poem.

By the eighteenth century the manuscript must have presented a
sadly dog-eared appearance, for it is then that it received its
leather binding with protective edges, after being trimmed down
to a comparatively neat finish. Tooling on the leather matches that
of other bindings from the monastery of Benediktbeuern, suggest-
ing that it had by this time found its destined home. As previously
noted, it was bound in the wrong order and with several sections
missing. Whether this was the fault of the binder or represented
the best he could make of an already bad job cannot now be
determined.

In 1803 a decree was issued ordering the secularization of
ecclesiastical property. The commission covering Benediktbeuern
was headed by Johann Christoph, Baron of Aretin. His attention
was soon drawn to an uncatalogued book-hoard kept at the
monastery in a separate department from its official library,
perhaps embodying a sort of *index librorum prohibitorum* includ-
ing Protestant and other heretical writings. He is reported to have
taken a particular fancy to this manuscript – no doubt for its
satires on church corruption, for he has been described as 'a true
son of the Age of Reason' – and to have carried it about with him
while he pursued the rest of his commission. When the treasures of
Benediktbeuern were moved to Munich, the manuscript was
stored in the Central Library (as it was then called), of which von
Aretin was appointed Chief Librarian in 1806.

Publication

The text of the *Carmina Burana* was first published in its entirety
– apart from the then undiscovered *Fragmenta* – in 1847. It was

edited and prepared for publication (and given its now common title) by Johann Andreas Schmeller of the Munich Central Library. The edition was republished in facsimile in 1938 and, despite its deficiencies, tends to be described by modern scholars as 'not entirely indispensable', or words to that effect.

Schmeller recognized that some sections had been wrongly bound and that others were missing, but made no apparent effort to establish the correct ordering of folios or to match up separated parts of the same songs. The folios of the manuscript are numbered in Schmeller's own pencilled handwriting from front to back as they come. As bound, 'folio 1' bears the miniature of Fortuna's Wheel and the songs *Fas et nefas* and *O Fortuna*. The genuinely earliest part of the manuscript was later shown to be the folio numbered 43, which begins with the last few lines of *Manus ferens munera*. This song has since been reconstructed from other sources, but it is not known how much unrecoverable text might have preceded it.

When the text is arranged in the right order it falls into four or five distinct sections which are now headed, respectively, Moral/ Satirical, Love Songs, Drinking and Gaming Songs, Religious Drama, and a Supplement. Though he failed to make that arrangement, Schmeller did recognize that certain pieces fell naturally together. His approach was to divide the whole into two, labelled respectively *Seria* ('serious things') and *Amatoria: Potatoria: Lusoria*. All the pieces he regarded as 'serious' – including the rambunctious 'Archpoet's Confession' – went into the first half, and in the printed text were numbered by him in Roman numerals, as opposed to the Arabic numerals he used for the comparatively frivolous pieces of the remainder. Certain passages which he deemed unsuitable for tender eyes were omitted from the main body of the text and relegated to the last page, where they are printed in type so small that only tender eyes are capable of reading them.

The presentation and layout of material in the 1847 edition can be criticized. That verse is written as prose in the manuscript does not help matters, but either Schmeller paid scant attention to the significance of various treatments of initials, or he failed to recognize the strict but varied forms (especially sequences) to which many of the pieces had been moulded. Issue can be taken with his readings of certain unclear words and passages, and with his corrections to (or sometimes failure to recognize) undoubted errors in the original. Many of these, however, even now remain the subject of debate, and Schmeller was conscientious enough to mark his modifications with inverted commas in the text and explanatory notes in an appendix. In this respect his corrections are more readily discernible than those of the modern text now taken as standard.

The correct order of folios was eventually established by Wilhelm Meyer, also of the Munich Central Library, who devoted over twenty years to research on the manuscript and its contents. (The task involved such painstaking procedures as matching up bookworm holes from one section to another.) As a by-product of this achievement he was able to show that certain folios and even whole sections were missing, and that the contents were therefore incomplete. He then sifted through all the library's material of Buranian origin with a view to discovering some of the missing folios. The seven folios that emerged from this quest (six between Schmeller's ff. 106 and 107, one following f. 112) were subsequently published under the title *Fragmenta Burana*.

Further treatments of the text were made by R. Peiper and L. Laistner. Peiper published his selection of songs from the Codex under the title *Gaudeamus! Carmina vagorum selecta in usum laetitiae* in 1877 and also prepared in manuscript a complete new edition of the whole text. Laistner's German verse translations of a selection originally published under the title *Golias: Studentenlieder des Mittelalters* (Stuttgart, 1879) were based on his own critical readings. Laistner's text has recently been republished under the title *Carmina Burana: Lateinisch und Deutsch: Lieder der Vaganten*.

The authoritative modern edition of the *Çarmina Burana* occupies four books, has been nearly fifty years in the making, and is still incomplete. Volume I contains the text itself, together with

textual notes. Part 1, *Moral and Satirical Poems*, was edited by
Alfons Hilka and Otto Schumann and appeared in 1930. Part 2,
Love Songs, edited chiefly by Schumann following the death of
Hilka, appeared in 1941. Part 3, *Drinking and Gaming Songs:
Religious Plays: Supplements*, appeared in 1970 under the edi-
torship of Bernhard Bischoff, Schumann having died in 1950.

Volume II was planned as a commentary on the text with an
introduction to the study of the manuscript itself. Part 1, contain-
ing Schumann's introduction and study of the handwriting, fol-
lowed by a commentary on the moral-satirical poems by himself
and Hilka, appeared in 1930. Parts 2 and 3 are still eagerly
awaited.

These volumes constitute what is generally referred to as the
'critical edition' of the *Carmina Burana* – a self-explanatory
description whose exact significance may be easily overlooked.
One might reasonably have expected the editors to reproduce the
actual text of the manuscript with as much fidelity as is consistent
with literary sense – that is to say (since the manuscript is partly
missing, partly damaged and in many places obviously corrupt),
with clearly marked emendations to the text where to leave it as it
stands would threaten confusion, unintelligibility, or incomplete-
ness. What the editors have in fact explicitly undertaken is to
reconstruct the presumed correct versions of what must have
appeared in the original sources used by the compilers of the
manuscript.

In many cases this has been made possible by comparison with
other manuscripts. Valuable results include the completion of
Manus ferens munera (CB 1), of which only the last few lines
remain in the manuscript, and of 'Phyllis and Flora', which breaks
off in mid-word at least sixteen and a half stanzas before the end
owing to the omission of a complete section from the bound
original. No less valuable has been the ability to compare so
lengthy and important a poem as the 'Archpoet's Confession'
with versions recorded in over thirty other manuscripts. This does
mean, however, that the text appearing in the critical edition is not
exactly that of the manuscript but an ideal composed from an

amalgam of all that seems best in three dozen different versions. And there is nothing in the main text to show where emendations have been made: variant readings and reasons for the final choice have to be painstakingly sifted from masses of accompanying footnotes, most of which (small print notwithstanding) occupy considerably more space than the text they purport to elucidate.

More seriously, the main text gives no indication of various omissions that have been made on the basis of editorial literary criticism. A controversial example is that of CB62, *Dum Diane vitrea*, which in manuscript consists of eight stanzas. Only four of these are printed as main text: the rest are relegated to the fine print of footnotes, together with Schumann's reasons for believing that they represent an insensitive, inconsequent and inconsistent accretion to what must have been the 'original' poem. Many scholars happen to agree with Schumann's judgement, but this does not answer what might be regarded as a question of literary ethics. If it is true that the *Codex Buranus* itself is, as medieval manuscripts go, particularly corrupt, it is equally arguable that the modern standard edition is not so much Platonic as bowdlerized.

Although commentaries on the text follow the bound folio numbering endorsed by Schmeller, his Roman–Arabic numbering system for individual pieces has been dropped, largely because it separates parts of songs which evidently go together. Modern editions now follow the numbering of items established in Hilka–Schumann–Bischoff, which is based on the reconstructed order of actual compilation. Thus *Fas et nefas*, though appearing on the first bound folio, is now numbered CB19. This would be a good system if every piece were numbered separately. Unfortunately, many pieces have the same number and are distinguished by an additional I and II or *a* and *b*, and in some cases it has since been shown that certain items so numbered are in fact not related.

The most convenient modern copy of the text is that published by the Deutscher Taschenbuch Verlag (see Bibliography). It compresses into one volume parallel texts in Latin original and German verse translation (by Carl Fischer, with acknowledgements to the memory of Laistner wherever the latter has already discovered the only possible equivalent rhyme), together with an introduction and annotations by Günter Bernt. The text is almost entirely that of Hilka–Schumann–Bischoff, the few divergences being carefully listed.

No complete edition of the *Carmina Burana* has appeared in Britain or America, apart from a facsimile of the manuscript with an English-language introduction by Bernhard Bischoff (see Bibliography). The University of Reading has published a selection of thirty poems edited and annotated by P. G. Walsh, and others may be found in the *Oxford Book of Medieval Latin Verse*. More appear with accompanying verse translations by Symonds, Waddell and Whicher. For a summary and concordance of song-texts accessible in English-language editions, see Appendix E. The most accessible studies in English are by Peter Dronke on Latin lyrics and Olive Sayce on German (see Bibliography).

Contents

The contents of the *Carmina Burana* fall into five sections.

1. CB 1–55 are poems of a moral, religious and didactic nature now generally categorized under the heading 'Moral/Satirical'. They account for about 20 per cent of the extant text. CB 1, of which only the last lines are preserved, must have been preceded by an unknown quantity of other poems in the same category (possibly, it has been suggested, even by an entire section, perhaps devoted to hymns and religious poetry of a pious rather than satirical nature).

2. CB 56–186, collectively referred to as 'Love Songs', form the largest section of the manuscript, accounting for just under 50 per cent of actual text. The section was originally longer, for at least one gathering of folios is known to be missing.

3. CB 187–226 constitute the 'Drinking and Gaming Songs' and form about 12 per cent of the text.

4. A fourth category may be distinguished for the two religious

plays constituting CB227 and CB228. These bring the manuscript up to folio 106.

5. A fifth category may be distinguished for all supplementary material added at a later date from the main body. Most of this occupies folios 107–12 and the unbound *Fragmenta*. Following the Hilka–Schumann–Bischoff critical edition, supplementary pieces are numbered separately and distinguished from the main text by an asterisk. CB1*–26a* constitute about 15 per cent of the whole.

It would be misleading to add the numbers in the critical edition and conclude that the text consists of 254 distinct pieces, though the number is certainly not less. Some divisions are doubtful, and for various reasons many pieces are grouped under the same number.

The songs in the first three sections mostly fall into natural and obviously intended groups linked by form or subject – there are even some subject-headings in the first to make this explicit. But it is not always easy to spot the relationship between pieces that are evidently intended to be related: any proposed schema tends to throw up inconsistencies, and some pieces quite clearly appear in the 'wrong' place. Surprise diminishes when it is remembered that the anthology may have been months or years in the preparation and that not all the compilers' source material may have been available at the same time.

Schmeller, working in numerical disorder, provided his edition with a complicated table of thematic analysis. Schumann, in the introduction to his Commentary (Vol. II, Part 1), offers an analysis of the thematic groups and lists them in the order in which they appear. A somewhat looser suggestion is made by Bischoff in his introduction to the facsimile edition:

Perhaps one may characterize the plan of the collection . . . somewhat differently: whenever the compiler of the songs came across something suitable, he included it, and the result was a collection of songs with moral and didactic annotations. Thus the schema of the *Carmina Burana*, strange as it may seem, approaches somewhat the plan of one or other of the moralizing encyclopedias which copiously quoted mediaeval rhymes and verses.

I Complaints and Satires

Most of the songs in the first section fit the customary but unwieldy heading 'Moral/Satirical'. (The critical edition's subtitle *Moralisch-satirische Dichtungen* does not sound much better in German.) 'Satire' here carries its original sense of social criticism and denunciation. It may be witty, but it is constructive rather than destructive and does not bear the overtones of parody and burlesque which we now tend to associate with it. (Parody appears as a genre in its own right in the appropriate surroundings of the drinking and gaming songs.) The medieval satirists' literary models are Juvenal and Horace, with a marked preference for the vituperation of the former over the urbanity of the latter.

These pieces exhibit a wide range of themes, forms and lengths, but are not entirely haphazard: to a large extent they fall into natural thematic groupings, some of which are underlined by introductory headings in the manuscript. Most are rhythmic as opposed to quantitive, and many are in sequence form. The few which are written in classical metres – including some taken from classical authors – tend to fall at the end of the thematic groups to which they belong. This suggests some underlying formal purpose on the part of the compilers – indeed, Schumann detects an element of scribal pride in the arrangement and balance of similar or contrasting pieces.

CB 1 to CB 13 attack the immorality of the times in general and of the clergy in particular. Simony is frequently singled out; its original meaning extended from the sale of church offices to the practice, at all levels of the ecclesiastical hierarchy, of charging for the exercise of priestly functions. The lay equivalent is avarice, which comes in for a good deal of attention. CB 6, *Florebat olim studium*, starts by deploring diminishing standards of education and goes on to compare the present generation unfavourably with that of – presumably – the author.

Variety in style and form can be well illustrated from this first group. CB1, *Manus ferens munera*, is cast in a finely wrought verse form: its expression is pointed and evident delight is taken in the working-out of virtually untranslatable grammatical puns. CB6 sounds an apocalyptic note in tub-thumping octosyllables beginning:

> *Ecce sonat in aperto*
> *vox clamantis in deserto:*
> *nos desertum, nos deserti,*
> *nos de pena sumus certi.*

> Hear the voice of one come crying
> from the wilderness outlying:
> we, deserters and deserted,
> hear our just deserts asserted.

The expression is blunt rather than pointed, though even this literary desert seems to be inhabited by puns.

A contrast to intellectual convolution and fundamentalist passion is provided by the metrical verses, which sound calmer, even aloof, as in CB7:

> *Nobilis est ille,*   *quem virtus nobilitavit;*
> *Degene est ille,*   *quem virtus nulla beavit.*

> Noble is he who has been ennobled by virtue:
> base that man whom no virtue has ever blessed.

CB14 to CB17 are concerned with the fickleness of Fate, including two songs well known from Orff: *Fortune plango vulnera* and *O Fortuna / velut luna*. Fortuna, though not unknown to the Romans, is one of several characters achieving greater prominence in the medieval pantheon: others include Nummus, equivalent to Mammon, and Decius, the dice god. Even Amor (Cupid) tends to overshadow Venus.

These are followed by further enquiries into the meaning of virtue. A humorous answer is provided by Walter of Châtillon in his begging poem *Fas et nefas* (CB 19), and a classical response by Horace, Ovid, Juvenal and others in the four metrical pieces constituting CB 20. Theirs reflect on the notion of the Golden Mean:

> *Virtus est medium vitiorum utrimque reductum.*

> Virtue lies at a point midway between two opposite vices.

Further sermons, admonitions and proverbs follow in more or less regular succession, up to CB 45. Three are introduced as *De correctione hominum* (CB 26–8), and these are followed by three poems by Peter of Blois and a set of proverbs under the heading *De conversione hominum* (CB 29–32). The section beginning CB 33 is preceded by the phrase *De ammonitione prelatorum*. Not all are addressed directly to or deal specifically with the 'prelates' who are being 'admonished': CB 38 and CB 40 are, again, proverbs in classical metre, but CB 37, *In Gedeonis area*, is unusually specific, relating to internal disputes which plagued the Benedictine monastery of Grandmont in the 1180s. CB 44 is an ecclesiastical parody, a prose satire known as 'The Gospel according to the Silver Mark'.

CB 46 to CB 55, which conclude the section, are said to be 'about' the crusades, *De cruce signatis*. They range widely from the historical, such as CB 47 on the fall of Jerusalem, to the incidental; CB 48 A is a terse but touching alba, i.e. a dawn song of lovers parting at daybreak.

The last pieces are an incantation (CB 54, *Omne genus demoniorum*) and two lines of untranslatable gobbledegook which may be a charm:

> *Amara tanta tyri   pastos sycalos sycalari*
> *Ellivoli scarras   polili posylique lyvarras.*

II Love Songs

The longest division of the *Carmina Burana* opens with the phrase *Incipiunt iubili*, 'Here begin the sequences.' The sequence is a verse form based on a sequence of paired stanzas, such that both stanzas of a pair follow exactly the same pattern of lines, line length and rhymes, but a new pattern is forged for each pair. Although derived from ecclesiastical antiphony, the sequence form had become popular for secular songs and poems, so that the phrase *Incipiunt iubili* would not just have referred to the type of verses to follow but also have suggested a change from religious to secular content. (Ironically so, since the same phrase appears in medieval church services to opposite effect. But parody may be suspected.) All but one of the first group of love songs are in fact sequences; thereafter, sequences remain typical but sporadic.

The section is incomplete, an unknown quantity of titles having been lost at some stage in the manuscript's history. Like the previous section, it features verse forms of all types, including some in classical metre. There are no subject headings, but the contents fall into natural groups by either theme or form. Some 85 per cent of them centre on love in all its manifestations, the remainder consisting chiefly of spring songs and dance songs. It has been suggested that 'the sorrows of love is the commonest theme', but closer examination shows that practically half the songs express the enjoyment of love either specifically or in general, while another quarter are wooing songs which presumably imply some hope of success – otherwise, why bother to embark upon them?

Considerable interest attaches to the large number of German-language songs and poems appearing in this section, so many of them unknown from any other source. The forty-seven German verses include love songs, spring songs and dance songs, and range in length from four to fourteen lines. Most act as appendices to Latin lyrics of two or more strophes, as the scribes have indicated by an intermediate hierarchical treatment of initial letters (and as the critical edition indicates by giving them the same numbers followed by *a*). The relationship is not always obvious. In some cases the German reflects, summarizes or extends the content of the preceding Latin; in many, it follows much the same rhythmic pattern and would therefore be singable to the same melody. They are not all complete: a few are single strophes from otherwise well-known lyrics. Some are of unknown antiquity and may be the last survivors of a pre-literate tradition; others are by twelfth-century lyricists such as Neidhart von Reuenthal and Walther von der Vogelweide. Many seem to be *ad hoc* compositions by the compiler and suggested by the associated Latin verses. In at least one case (CB 149, *Floret silva nobilis*) the rather clumsy Latin verse is evidently modelled on the more polished German.

Several genres may be illustrated from this section. The pastourelle (Prov. *pastorela*) recounts an amorous encounter between a country girl, typically a shepherdess, and a transient man of the world, who may be a knight, a scholar, a troubadour. He attempts to seduce her, usually – or at least initially – by persuasion rather than force, and may or may not succeed. Quite often he fails, and the girl is shown to be more than a match for him in the arts of argument. The alba (a Provençal form for which the later French equivalent is the aubade) is a dawn song depicting the sorrowful parting of lovers at daybreak, usually alerted to it by a sympathetic herald or watchman.

The debate was a structure much enjoyed by medieval writers. Notable examples in the *Carmina Burana* are those between Phyllis and Flora (CB 92) and Wine and Water (CB 193), while the form also underlies the beautiful seduction poem *Estatis florigero tempore* (CB 70). Another literary device prominent in this section is that of the 'nature introduction' to love songs, whereby thoughts of love are induced by the onset of spring. Sometimes the poet dwells more on nature than on its inevitable accompaniment. We are reminded that winter was as cold and uncomfortable indoors as out, and that privacy was a rare bloom, to be plucked only in woods and wild places. We may not be surprised to learn that summer really was better in those days, as Europe basked in a climatic optimum lasting into the thirteenth century. (Is it, then, surprising that some of the most beautiful lyrics of the time are winter poems? The present collection ends on a wintry note.)

CB 56 to CB 96 are mainly about love and consist of sequences, lays and regularly patterned verses with refrains. The first of them, *Ianus annum circinat*, is typical. Though written in the first person, the person is universal rather than individual: the *persona* takes precedence over the (anonymous) poet. Its five verses may be summarized thus: (1) spring has returned; (2) the prospect of love banishes winter gloom; (3) I have my eye on a particular beauty; (4) I burn with love: she is perfection; (5) let me live long enough to win her. A two-line refrain affirms the omnipotence of love: *Vincit Amor omnia, / regit Amor omnia.*

Most of the songs in this section follow a similar pattern, though with the emphasis variously apportioned between the elements of nature and love, and with differing degrees of subjectivity (not all are in the first person). But there are some notable exceptions. CB 62, *Dum Diane vitrea*, is a nocturne primarily in praise of sleep, which is pictured first as an antidote to love and later as a welcome attendant in its train. Two consecutive pieces, CB 76 and CB 77, are both in goliardic verse and both appear to express personal experience, but in subject matter could hardly contrast more sharply: *Dum caupona verterem* recounts an adventure in a brothel, whereas *Si linguis angelicis* presents an ecstatic, quasi-religious vision of love requited. CB 92, also in goliardic verse and by far the longest song in the collection, is the famous debate between Phyllis and Flora – known from many other sources – as to whether preference attaches to the love of a cleric or that of a knight. There are two pieces in the manner of a pastourelle, including the incomplete *Exiit diluculo* (CB 90), while CB 89, *Nos duo boni*, suggests a pastourelle at first sight but on closer examination proves to be an obscure philosophical debate between two shepherds and a shepherdess. Only two sets of metrical verses appear: one on the labours of Hercules and another on the steeds of Apollo (CB 66, *Acteon, Lampos*, etc.). CB 91, *Sacerdotes, mementote*, seems the most out-of-place item in this section, belonging thematically to the moral/satirical part of the anthology.

CB 97 to CB 102 recount unhappy love stories from the classics, notably those of Dido and Aeneas and of Helen and Paris.

Unhappiness in love remains the principal topic of CB 103 to CB 120, practically all in the first person and recounted as if from the life. Many are sequences, the remainder chiefly in regular verse with or without refrain. Four are verses in German.

CB 121, *Tange, sodes, citharam*, is an uninhibited expression of joy in a love that seems very much requited, and all the more welcome for appearing out of place – perhaps deliberately, for contrast?

CB 122 to CB 134 are a mixture of pieces of which only one relates to love, and that in an unusual and moving way. *Huc usque, me miseram!* (CB 126) is the lament of a pregnant girl whose lover has 'been forced to flee' to a foreign country by the scandal – at least, that is her more than charitable explanation of his disappearance, whatever we may be led to think about it from reading between the lines. CB 128, *Remigabat naufragus*, appears to be a poem of thanksgiving for rescue from a shipwreck. Allegory may be strongly suspected, and a perhaps homosexual experience obliquely referred to. Whether this counts as 'love' is a moot point.

'Sad stories of the death of kings' might appropriately subtitle some of the songs in this batch, including that of Philip of Swabia, murdered in 1208 (CB 124, *Dum Philippus moritur*), and possibly Richard the Lionheart, killed in a siege in 1199 (CB 122, *Expirante primitivo*). Others are classifiable as 'laments', but not all to any serious degree: *Olim lacus colueram* (CB 130) is the original swan-song, supposedly sung from the serving-dish on which the said bird lies stiff and flightless:

> *Miser, miser –*
> *modo niger*
> *et ustus fortiter!*

> Poor thing, poor thing –
> not a raw thing
> but done like anything!

CB 135 to CB 161 fall into the pattern of seasonal introduction – spring and early summer are hardly differentiated – followed by expressions of love enjoined, enjoyed or lamented as the case may be.

CB 161a is a summer frolic with no mention of love, CB 162 a jolly student song.

At CB 163 a cloud seems to pass overhead: from here to CB 175 love is taken neat, undiluted by 'nature introductions', and the topic is generally approached in a less joyful frame of mind. Laments abound of unrequited love, accompanied by expressions of desire often uncoloured by any certainty of a favourable response. Two of the German verses have a winter setting.

CB 177 to CB 186, which conclude the love songs, are a mixture of pieces. It would be hard to find a greater contrast than between CB 177, *Stetit puella* – half Latin, half German, short, sweet, irregular and ingenuous – and CB 178, *Volo virum vivere* – one of the few genuine 'courtly love' poems of the collection, long, sour, highly controlled and ingenious. CB 180, *O mi dilectissima*, can be read as happy or sad, depending on one's interpretation of the haunting and not entirely meaningful refrain *Mandaliet! Mandaliet! / Min geselle chumet niet!* CB 183, *Si puer cum puellula*, is frankly ribald; yet attached to it is CB 183a, *Ich sich den morgensterne brechen* ('I see the Morning Star arise') – an alba, or dawn song, in praise of secret love. CB 185 recounts a seduction in mixed Latin and German from the girl's viewpoint (*Ich was ein chint so wolgetan*, 'O what a lovely girl I was!'), and the section concludes with *Suscipe, Flos, florem*, a dignified avowal of love in that medieval transformation of classical metre known as leonine verse.

Nearly all the contents of the section comply with the 'love' heading, or at least are erotic, and those that do not are about nature or other 'romantic' subjects. In accordance with age-old tradition, love is often represented by the metaphor of flame or fire. No less commonly it is regarded as an illness or pain which only the beloved can cure, even (for example, in CB 66, *Si linguis angelicis*) as a wound which can only be healed by 'the one who has dealt it'. Love-wounds are also caused by Cupid, who is depicted in CB 87, *Amor tenet omnia*, as hovering everywhere and incessantly shooting off his darts. Love is not, however, regarded as the madness often referred to by classical authors.

It is personified in several characters from myth and legend, especially Venus (rarely in her Greek guise as Aphrodite). She is often associated with and sometimes eclipsed by her son Cupid, occasionally under his Greek name, Eros, but more frequently under his preferred medieval name, Amor. Tragic love is represented by Dido and Aeneas, the enjoyment of love by Paris, the power of attraction by Helen – whom, however, medieval poets tend to regard unfavourably as a temptress.

Feminine beauty is described (habitually from the top downwards) by reference to hair, eyes, cheeks, mouth, face or figure in general, sometimes breasts, and rarely anything else except in particularly erotic verse (such as CB 83). An apparent lack of ears has been ascribed to their concealment by hair or headdress, but this leaves unexplained a conspicuous absence of noses. Favoured colours are gold for hair, and red or white for various other parts of the visible anatomy, with red representing passion and white purity. The beloved is often likened to a rose; indeed, *Rosa* and *Flos* are often used as generic terms. Phyllis and Flora themselves are, at root, botanically named.

Few of the songs can be classified as full-blooded representatives of the courtly love tradition, but many reflect its conventions, and the usual word for love in German verse, *Minne*, is basically the courtly species of *Liebe*. A convention frequently referred to, sometimes, obliquely, is that of the 'five stages of love' through which the development of intimacy passes. The stages may be reduced to four, and the headings are not always the same, but they are amusingly made explicit in a song about 'little Cecily'

(CB 88, *Amor habet superos*, not included in the present selection) as follows:

> *Volo tantum ludere,*
> *id est: contemplari,*
> *presens loqui, tangere,*
> *tandem osculari;*
> *quintum, quod est agere,*
> *noli suspicari!*

> I only wish to flirt a little –
> i.e., gaze upon her,
> peradventure talk with her,
> touch, and even kiss her.
> As to what comes fifth – performance –
> nothing could be further . . . !

Ludere is the usual verb for to flirt, dally or, more literally, play around with, and the five stages listed here may be expressed in English as (1) eye-to-eye contact (*contemplari*), (2) sweet converse (*loqui*), (3) touching – perhaps just holding hands (*tangere*), (4) kissing (*osculari*), (5) congress (*agere*). A frequent courtly metaphor, or rather euphemism, for consummation is *solacium*, 'solace' – which brings us back to the notion of love as pain or physical disorder.

III Drinking and Gaming Songs

The contents of the third section are numbered CB 187–226 and total forty-five pieces, counting separately the supernumeraries designated 'a'. About three-quarters fit the drinking/gaming description more or less adequately, the rest being mainly moral and satirical. One-third are metrical verses headed *versus* as in the first section. There are two prose pieces, one in rhymed prose, one song in German and one macaronic in Latin and German.

CB 187 to CB 192 belong thematically to the 'moral/satirical' section of the manuscript, with the possible exception of CB 191 *Estuans intrinsecus* – the so-called 'Archpoet's Confession'. Regarded as one of the greatest poems of the Middle Ages and known from more manuscripts than any other in this collection, *Estuans* certainly has all the appearance of a repentance, bringing to mind that of *Dum iuventus floruit* (CB 30) in the first section of the manuscript. But the life-style of wenching, gaming and drinking is here described with such gusto, not to mention wit and reason, as to sound in the final analysis more like a confession 'to' than 'of'.

CB 193 to CB 206 relate to food, drink and conviviality, including the parodic 'debate' between wine and water – CB 193, *De conflictu vini et aque* – and the rousing tavern song, *In taberna quando sumus* (CB 196).

CB 207 to CB 210 relate specifically to chess and dicing, one of them – CB 210, *Qui cupit egregium* – purporting to instruct the reader in the ways of the former. Several of the accompanying miniatures illustrate games popular at the time, showing also backgammon. One of them has a patterned background reminiscent of suit symbols, though it antedates the introduction of playing-cards by more than a century.

Other themes and genres are notable in this section. One of four begging poems, CB 191a, *Cum sit fama multiplex*, formally resembles its immediate precursor, the 'Archpoet's Confession', but is not now thought to bear any significant connection: it would have been better numbered separately. Two consecutive songs are student calls to celebration: CB 215, *Tempus hoc letitie*, is followed by CB 216, *Iocundemur, socii* (threatening to evoke the response *Iuvenes dum sumus*). A similar piece, *Omittamus studia*, appears as CB 75, out of place, as it were, in the previous section.

Parody is rife. CB 197, *Dum domus lapidea*, vaguely parallels CB 62, *Dum Diane vitrea*, thereby incidentally attesting to the popularity of its target. The Archpoet's parody of a Confession is matched by a parody of the Mass for gamesters and gamblers (CB 215, *Officium lusorum*), and this by CB 219, *Cum 'In orbem universum'*, which outlines the rules of the supposedly latest monastic order – *Ordo Vagarum*, the Order of Tramps, or Wandering Scholars if you prefer. (Its title is a later addition to the manuscript.)

CB 222, *Ego sum abbas Cucaniensis*, may be satire with a particular target in view, or be equally well regarded as liturgical parody. There follow metrical verse proverbs harking back to moral themes explored in earlier sections, and two begging poems. The section ends at CB 226 with the satire *De mundi statu*, a global 'state of the nation' address which might have been more at home in the moral/satirical section.

IV The Religious Dramas

Drama, discountenanced by the Church, paradoxically developed within it, where it could be kept under control. Emerging from those services in the Christian calendar with obvious dramatic appeal, such as Easter and Christmas, the religious dramas that have come down to us may be characterized as liturgy supplemented by additional material in prose and verse from secular sources.

CB 227 is a Christmas play which starts with the announcement of Jesus's birth and concludes with the death of Herod and the angel's advice to flee into Egypt. CB 228 amounts to a long poem with parts spoken or sung by the King of Egypt, Mary and Joseph. As drama it is probably the fragment of something more substantial: parts of it seem borrowed from a known drama about the Antichrist.

The other dramas come from the *Fragmenta Burana* and are therefore numbered with the Supplement. CB 13* is a comparatively short passion play in some thirty-three lines of prose; CB 15* a resurrection play in prose and (mainly) verse; CB 16* a longer passion play in Latin and German verse and prose, with biblical and liturgical text. Verses set in the Orff cantata beginning *Chramer, gip die varwe mier* are spoken by Mary Magdalene at an early point in the play – 'Chapman, let me have some rouge / made for my complexion: / so that I may lead young men / willy-nilly / into my affection.'

CB26* dramatizes the appearance of Jesus to his disciples on the road to Emmaus, and CB26a* the ascension of Mary.

V Supplement

Twenty-six items are regarded as supplemental. CB1* to CB6* are written over or beside songs in the main body of the text, CB7* to CB15* occupy folios I to VI of the *Fragmenta*, CB16* to CB25* are found in folios 107–12, and CB26 and CB26a* are in folio VII of the *Fragmenta*. All are of later date than the main body, including those on the folios bound in with it (107–12).

This miscellany includes five of the religious dramas mentioned above and a number of hymns and prayers, several in praise of St Catherine. There are also some poems ascribed with greater or lesser certitude to der Marner, notably CB3* and CB6*. The former is a winter poem modelled on one (in German) by Walther von der Vogelweide, the latter a poem dating from 1230–1 in praise of Heinrich von Maria Saal, Bishop of Seckau.

CB8* is a repeat of CB111, *O comes amoris dolor*, but with additional stanzas.

Authorship

Who composed the *Carmina Burana*? Few songs in the manuscript are ascribed to anyone by name, and few known names of the time can be attached with certainty to any of the songs. So widely do they range in subject, style, treatment and literary interest that the number of writers represented is clearly large.

Certain generalizations can be made. That the writers form an educated elite is apparent from the very fact of composition rather than from the choice of Latin as their medium. But their fluent Latinity, academic tastes and generally reflective tone place them close to the roots of their education: they are still students, recent graduates, or men whose position keeps them in contact with scholastic circles.

In short, the songs are written by scholars. They are popularly supposed to have been written by scholars described as 'wandering', but this tends to upset modern scholars with more sedentary proclivities. In fact, the term is right in one sense and misleading in another. It is right to the extent that all scholars at this period of history were inclined to wander. The roads of Europe were full of students travelling from one centre of learning to another: and not only students but also teachers, who could quite satisfactorily set up an informal school at any town of their choice if they proved popular enough to attract a following. One would even encounter the teacher and his class in transit together – *magistrum cum pueris* – as suggested by CB 219. It was in this way that so many scholars of the time, from Abélard down, gained and enhanced their reputations. Men of learning and academic substance also passed from country to country to take up appointments at courts and chancelleries, unhindered by the modern iniquity of passport and customs control, and facilitated by fluency in the international language of Latin.

In the more specific and objectionable sense, wandering scholars are associated with bands of academic drop-outs and spoiled priests gone wild, who did indeed wander from place to place, monopolizing the taverns, upsetting the locals and generally plaguing the authorities by their antisocial behaviour. These people were known as goliards, the disciples and followers of a legendary bishop-turned-songster called Golias. (Golias is a form of Goliath, who in Christian mythology had assumed devilish proportions.) They are represented as raucous, bawdy and bibulous, delighting in the composition and recital of clever but scurrilous tavern songs favouring wine, women, gaming and the delights of the open road, and mocking degenerate priests, disapproving monks, and self-righteous supporters of what we should now call the Establishment. Even a verse form appropriate to their theme is described as goliardic:

> Cum 'In orbem universum'   decantatur 'ite',
> sacerdotes ambulant,   currunt cenobite . . .

> 'Go ye into all the world . . .'
>   hear the text – it's stunning!
> Simple clerics saunter up,
>   novices come running . . .

Some of the *carmina Burana* clearly conform to the goliardic ideal, especially (and not surprisingly) those of the section headed 'Drinking and Gaming Songs'; but many more do not, and it would be going too far to characterize the anthology *in toto* as a wandering scholars' song-book. Even had it been widely available, none of them could have afforded it.

Of the few nameable authors of *carmina Burana*, perhaps Hugh of Orléans most nearly approaches the wandering ideal – an ideal which renders unsurprising a paucity of biographical detail about him, other than the verse anecdotes he recounts about himself, his friends and his more numerous enemies. He was born in 1093, presumably at Orléans, where he died in 1160. He studied at Paris and spent the rest of his life apparently roaming France but with frequent visits to his native city – whether for love or money one can only speculate. His ingeniously rhymed church satires and down-to-earth verses on wine, women and song were of such power and originality as to earn him the nickname Primas – 'the Master'. Later goliardic writers were to take him as a model, even to associate him with the nebulous figure of Golias himself.

By way of contrast, Peter of Blois (1135–1212) led an ordered and well-established life. Secretary to Henry II of England until the latter's death in 1189, he then settled in Paris as a teacher of grammar to English students, and eventually finished his career as Archdeacon of Bath. Amongst ten or so of the poems ascribable to him in the anthology are CB72, *Grates ago Veneri*, describing a forceful seduction, and CB 30, *Dum iuventus floruit*, a song of conversion from youthful folly to pious maturity.

Walter of Châtillon (1135–1204) was a native of Lille and studied at Paris, Rheims and Bologna before settling as a teacher in the town with which his name is associated. He, too, served under Henry II, later becoming secretary to the Archbishop of Rheims. Some half-dozen of his works appear in the *carmina*, including the first in the collection (*Manus ferens munera*) and the witty begging-poem, CB 19, *Fas et nefas*. Though now best remembered for his moral and satirical poems attacking the higher clergy, he also wrote seriously on theological topics and was renowned in his time as the author of a Latin epic on Alexander the Great. He died of leprosy.

Attempts have been made, without success, to detect the hand of Breton-born Peter Abélard (1079–1142) in the Buranian anthology. His youthful love songs achieved such popularity in the streets of Paris – and not only amongst students – that he later found them an embarrassment. For his attempts to reconcile Catholic faith to God-given reason – or vice versa – Abélard is accounted one of the greatest scholars of the Middle Ages, and commanded sufficient renown in his own time to attract students from all over Europe to his classes at the embryonic University of Paris. Yet his life was as blighted as it was blessed. In 1116 he eloped with his private pupil Héloïse, who had been in the care of her uncle the Canon Fulbert, and who bore him a son at his family estate in Brittany. Returned to Paris, he was attacked and castrated by Fulbert's minions. Héloïse, as we have seen (p. 14), retired to a nunnery and eventually became abbess of a convent founded by her husband. Despite (or perhaps because of) his renown, Abélard attracted the opprobrium of the anti-intellectual Bernard of Clairvaux, who twice succeeded in having him condemned by ecclesiastical councils and barred from teaching. Abélard survived his second condemnation by only two years.

The greatest figure in medieval Latin literature belongs to the German-speaking world and is known only by the nickname claimed by himself and endorsed by his contemporaries and everyone since. 'The Archpoet' seems to have occupied the position of Poet Laureate to his patron Rainald of Dassel (d. 1165). Chaplain to Barbarossa, Rainald was promoted to Chancellor in 1154, and in 1156 became Archbishop of Cologne. To him is addressed CB 191, *Estuans intrinsecus*, the so-called 'Archpoet's Confession', an ambiguously moral self-exposé whose popularity is attested by the number of medieval manuscripts in which it is reproduced (with varying degrees of fidelity). Little is known of this remarkable poet, beyond the tantalizing dashes of self-portraiture that emerge from the ten surviving works of undisputed authorship. In *The Wandering Scholars*, Helen Waddell devotes a chapter to sketching a romantic outline of the man whom she describes as 'a ghost, but a ghost with a cough'. She continues, by way of explanation: 'He is coughing in the first lyric we have from him, dated from internal evidence and much patient research about 1161, a dramatic cough, that suggests the gift of a cloak: and he is coughing in the last, safe housed in St Martin's cloister at Cologne.' The earlier words in question are:

> *Tussis indificiens   et defectus vocis . . .*

> By coughing weakened   and with feeble voice . . .

The *carmina Burana* include several poems by great German lyric poets: three by Reinmar der Alte (*fl.* 1180–90), one by Heinrich von Morungen (*fl.* 1190–1200), four by Walther von der Vogelweide (*c.* 1170–1228). Amongst other known authors are the monk Otloh of St Emmeram (CB 28, *Laudat rite Deum*); Bishop Marbod of Rennes (1035–1123); Godfrey, Prior of Winchester (d. 1107); Godfrey of St Victor (d. about 1194); Dietmar von Aist (mid-twelfth century); Neidhart von Reuenthal (early thirteenth century); and Der Marner (d. about 1267). Some of the verses are shown (by Olive Sayce in *The Medieval German Lyric 1150–1300*) to have been written by one or other of the scribes responsible for the compilation. CB 149, for instance, *Floret silva nobilis*, is evidently a translation modelled on the accompanying German verse, *Gruonet der walt allenthalben*.

The Translations

My original aim in translating the *carmina Burana* was not to compose poetry deriving from medieval inspiration but to produce equivalent English verse singable to the Orff cantata. For this purpose it was essential to reproduce as closely as possible the metre, rhythm, rhyme scheme and stanzaic forms of the Latin selection. On turning my attention to the rest of the text I found it expedient to retain this approach – partly for the sake of consistency ('the hobgoblin of little minds' – Emerson), and largely because by nature I find the technicalities of verse a more tractable challenge than the abstractions of poetry. In which connection a line from Jean-Luc Godard's *Alphaville* comes to mind – on poetry: 'You think it's secrets, but it turns out to be nothing.'

This should not be interpreted as a disclaimer of responsibility for the tone or emotional effect of the resultant English verse. As it is impossible to translate poetry literally or objectively, the following renderings must be taken for what they are: a translation of a personal response to the originals – the response of a person of a particular age, sex, nationality, generation, background, training, bias and predilection – and not necessarily of the poetic content of the originals themselves. For an analytic assessment of the original Latin, read any of the critiques listed in the bibliography. For a more valid subjective assessment, read the original Latin.

Most medieval Latin verse is stress-rhythmic, like English verse, and not quantitive like that of the classical authors. (They borrowed the habit from Greek, a language to which it was always more appropriate.) The *carmina Burana* included a number of pieces in classical metre, such as hexameters in CB20, *Est modus in verbis*, and elegiac couplets in CB210, *Qui cupit egregium*. In quantitive verse, the metrical units (feet) of each line are patterned by reference to long and short syllables as opposed to the stressed and slack of rhythmic verse. This does not work in English, and I have followed the obvious device of paralleling long syllables with stressed and short with slack, though I am fully aware of the technical deficiencies of the system. Where a classical foot may by convention be either a spondee (long, long) or a dactyl (long, short, short), I have chosen freely. In the hexametric one-line proverbs of Otloh (CB28, *Laudat rite Deum*) I found six feet excessive to the sense in English and replaced them all by iambic pentameters with an equivalent caesura.

Although rhyme played no part in the classical scheme except for occasional effect, medieval poets developed a transformation of the hexameter known as 'leonine verse', which characteristically rhymed at the half-line. An example from CB207, the verses on dicing:

> *Sunt comites ludi   mendacia, iurgia, nudi,*
> *Parva fides, furta,   macies, substantia curta.*

> Guess who accompany gaming? –
> Trickery, Trumpery, Shaming,
> Breaking-of-pledges, and Theft,
> and Having-no-property-left.

Just as the Christian Church evangelized in its own brand of Vulgar Latin rather than Classical, so it eschewed classical metre in favour of rhythmic verse, which had always been closer to the people. To this it added the device of rhyme, which, if not originating in, was at least facilitated by the vertical repetition of words bearing the same case-ending. The formal basis of medieval Latin lyric is founded on a long and rich tradition of Christian hymnody which may be traced back to St Ambrose in the fourth century.

Medieval poets took great delight in the formal aspects of their art, basically because most of it was designed to be sung, and song requires a degree of structural regularity. An early convention of troubadour poetry was the requirement for poet-composers to forge an entirely original verse form and melody for each new production. Increasing formal complexity was inevitable and a limit was bound to be reached, but out of them eventually crystallized a wide range of distinctive forms and genres of which some, such as the pastourelle and the ballade, would remain popular for centuries.

A predictable regularity of form proved particularly desirable for lyrics, partly because free verse does not lend itself to singing, and partly because, as a matter of practical entertainment, it was useful to be able to ring the changes between lyrics and melodies. A piece such as CB62, *Dum Diane vitrea*, is rare among the *carmina Burana* for the almost modern way in which each stanza is unique in form yet entirely appropriate to its content. It is in such instances that we observe the evolution of *carmina* = 'songs' to *carmina* = 'poems'. In this and comparable instances of deliberate irregularity – especially in 'sequences', best exemplified by CB72, *Grates ago Veneri* – I have closely paralleled the lines by syllable, stress, slack and rhyme, so that the form may be described as literally translated even if the words are not.

Although English and Medieval Latin verse are both rhythmic, attempting to reproduce the rhythm of one in verse of the other gives rise to a problem of compatibility. The structure of Latin is such that its natural verse rhythm is trochaic; that is, the line is a succession of trochees, which are feet consisting of a stressed syllable followed by a slack. It is well exemplified by the thirteenth-century hymn beginning:

> *Díes írae, díes ílla*
> *sólvet sáeclum cúm favílla . . .*

But the structure of English is such that its natural foot is iambic: its most typical line has feet ('iambs') consisting of a slack syllable followed by a stressed, as in:

> *The cúrfew tólls the knéll of párting dáy,*
> *The lówing hérd winds slówly ó'er the léa . . .*

English verse can be written in trochees, but the effect is rarely lyrical: more often it is staid (*Praise, my soul, the King of Heaven / To his feet thy tribute bring*), or primitive, as used to deliberate effect in *Hiawatha's Wedding-Feast*, or bitingly humorous, as in Lewis Carroll's parody, *Hiawatha's Photographing*:

> *But he opened out the hinges,*
> *Pushed and pulled the joints and hinges,*
> *Till it looked all squares and oblongs*
> *Like a complicated figure*
> *In the Second Book of Euclid.*

Trochees also tend to demand feminine rhymes, which in English are so intimately associated with humorous verse as to be dangerous in a serious context. Thus, when reading Medieval Latin trochaic verse, one has to be very careful not to be misled by connotations of humour which are part of the English experience but absent from the Latin subtext.

On the whole I decided not to convert trochaic originals into iambic equivalents, preferring wherever possible to let the underlying flavour of Medieval Latin percolate through the English lines. The result is chiefly effective in the more apocalyptic satires such as *Ecce sonat in aperto*, and rollicking pieces such as *In taberno quando sumus*. In pieces of sustained lyricism, however, such as 'Phyllis and Flora', I have compromised by alternating trochaic with iambic lines in an attempt to combine the authenticity of the former with the fluency of the latter.

Some Latin verses are themselves iambic, or occasionally dactylic, and here I have followed the originals. In a very few instances I have consciously changed the rhythm for one reason or another. Such departures are recorded in the Notes.

The contents of the *Carmina Burana* are full of puns, verbal pyrotechnics, parodies, resonances and cross-references to biblical, classical and contemporary popular literature. Wherever possible I have sought to match them with English equivalents. Resultant anachronisms may be taken as deliberate.

*

I should like to thank Graham Parlett, Paul Chown, John McLaughlin, and Françoise Tomlin for help within their various fields of expertise, and Tom and Margot Werneck for their hospitality in Munich. Thanks are also due to my patient wife for having so long accepted the *Carmina* as an excuse for opting out of life, and to the dedicatee for having introduced me to them in the first place – more years ago, as they say, than I care to remember.

Finally, I wish to record my debt to Betty Radice, who died while this book was in proof. Her enthusiasm was a constant source of encouragement and her criticisms were always right. She will be missed by many as an editor who inevitably became a friend.

SELECTED SONGS

I
Sermons and Satires

CB 1 Bribery and Corruption

Manus ferens munera
pium facit impium . . .

Hands with handsome gifts to wield
put the 'pi' in piety.
Money sees the compact sealed –
buys a court's propriety –
helps the adamantine yield –
smoothes out contrariety.
    Prelates' money-lust is
    all we know of justice:
    money gently nudges
    you who serve as judges.

Money being testified
makes a mockery of law:
equity, though on their side,
counts for nothing to the poor:
wealthy clients, quickly spied,
quicker still are catered for.
    Judges so adore it
    they'll move mountains for it:
    causes with it pleading
    find themselves succeeding.

Money when it comes along
bids fair play a fond farewell:
though the case be none too strong
curias say 'Bagatelle!
grease a palm – you can't go wrong –
chuck that pauper in a cell!'
    Laws are only made for
    those by whom they're paid for:
    not a one endorses
    men of no resources.

Money tends to gravitate
to the top dogs of their time:
offer cash commensurate
and, with courtesy sublime,
they'll apply the going rate
to eradicate your crime.
    Money, not vocation,
    marks the priestly station:
    manifest impostors
    preach us paternosters.

'Give, and gain a hundredfold:
hear the words of holy writ!' –
so the goodly giver's told
by the priestly hypocrite
to increase the latter's hold
on such paupers as submit.
    Life is for indulging
    if your purse is bulging –
    for it marks the measure
    of your paid-up pleasure.

Curias will gladly sway
cases gilded in advance:
poor old Codrus, truth to say,
wouldn't stand much of a chance:
thus the practice of the day
does but little to enhance
   all who ablatively
   tax us substantively:
   whose possessive yearnings
   feed off dative earnings.

CB2   Never Satisfied

Responde, qui tanta cupis . . .

'Tell me, unsatisfiable you' (I heard Generosity say)
'how much do you want? Whatever it is, I'll pay.'
'I'd just like my coffer filled.'
'Very well.'
  'Plus two more.'
    'There you are!'
      'Make it FOUR –
I think that should do.'
      'You! You're always the same:
no matter how much I give, you demand to increase it –
nor till the day you die do I reckon you'll cease it!'

CB 3   Mouldering Morals

Ecce torpet probitas,
virtus sepelitur . . .

Morals lie a-mouldering,
   virtue's all a-tatter,
liberality grows lean,
   parsimony fatter,
only lies are genuine —
   truth's another matter.
   Laws are for the breaking:
all illicitly allow
   any undertaking.

Mammon lords it over all,
   misers run the nation —
none but wouldn't gladly crawl
   for a small donation,
counting on their wherewithal
   for their reputation.
   Laws are for the breaking:
understanding underwrites
   any undertaking.

What's the hardest verb to learn?
   GIVE is. Give — gave — given.
Few words are of less concern
   to those who have striven
after wealth — who, more they earn,
   more to crave are driven.
   Laws are for the breaking:
moneymakers can't keep count
   of the amount they're making.

Self-control is on the wane,
    prurience uprears:
faithless vows are poured in vain
    into faithless ears:
Jove to Juno's found to feign,
    Dido to Aeneas.
    Laws are for the breaking:
who forsake fidelity
    are themselves forsaking.

If you seek to be precise
    don't describe as 'living'
fools who, once involved in vice,
    sin without misgiving.
Life? The word must ill suffice
    for their self-deceiving.
    Laws are for the breaking —
all overtly overlook
    any undertaking.

CB6   The World Upside Down

*Florebat olim studium
nunc vertitur in tedium . . .*

Once learning flourished. Now it's come
to be condemned as tedium:
the days of thirsting after truth
are now the idle days of youth.

For students hardly in their prime
find themselves wise before their time:
they know it all — impertinence
replaces plain intelligence.

In days gone by we were required
to stick with study: none retired,
or wished himself to be released,
till ninety years of age at least.

Now lads of barely a decade
can graduate – get themselves made
professors too! And who's to mind
how blind the blind who lead the blind?

So fledgelings soar upon the wing,
so donkeys play the lute and sing:
bulls dance about at court like sprites
and ploughboys sally forth as knights.

Down at the inn, Pope Gregory
is brawling ignominiously:
Jerome, austerest saint on earth,
goes haggling for a ha'pence-worth.

Augustine of his harvestings,
St Benedict of vinous things,
converse collusively – discreet
as a couple of fishwives in the street.

Reclining idly, Mary bores,
while Martha moans about her chores:
no movement stirs the womb of Leah,
and Rachel's flashing eyes look blear.

Stern Cato's tasteful rectitude
displays a new-found taste for food:
Lucretia's chaste virginity
is up for sale – or offered free.

Ideas our parents used to shun
shine in the eyes of everyone:
what's moist is now called dry, and what
once passed for cold now counts as hot.

Virtue's translated into vice,
hard work's considered not quite nice;
phenomena forget their place,
things fall apart, they leave no trace.

Now let the prudent man take care
to bring his soul to good repair –
lest at the last, when Death arraign,
he cry 'Lord, Lord!', and cry in vain –

For once that Judge has sentenced, He'll
convene no court of last appeal.

CB 10   A Voice in the Wilderness

Ecce sonat in aperto
vox clamantis in deserto . . .

Hark! The voice of one comes crying
from the wilderness outlying: –

We deserting, we deserted
hear our just deserts asserted:
life is nobody's ambition:
none but live in death's condition:
every one a sinner, traitor
to the plans of our creator:
none will bear his cross nor heed a
call to follow Christ as leader.

Who is good? Who trust-inspiring?
Who complies with God's requiring?
In a word, in brief opinion:
Death extends his dark dominion –
stalking those in priestly raiment
who extort unpriestly payment –
who, enrobed at ordination,
offer vows of dedication
which from well-lined benefices
they forswear as artifices:
in God's house their vice reposes –
stinking weeds instead of roses.
Holy they are not, but wholly
crooks who grind God's law down slowly.
Simon's one of that tradition,
seeking people of position:
Simon favours all who favour
Simon, be they ill of savour:
Simon, down at Rome invested,
leaves no cloister unmolested.
Keep a coin back, Simon's hateful –
grease his palm and Simon's grateful:
Simon stealing, Simon loaning –
here promoting, there dethroning –
leads this man to fear and falter,
that one to the wedding altar:
men once excommunicated
find themselves blessed and elated.
Simon makes no bones about it –
he'll confound law soon as flout it.
May that Simon be confounded
in whom so much power is grounded! –
May St Peter, losing patience,
cast him down to Hell's foundations.
He who spends his life high-flying
fits himself for Hell on dying.

Who would share this same addiction
let him share the same affliction –
sepulchred infernally
expiate eternally!

CB 16   Hard Luck

Fortune plango vulnera
stillantibus ocellis . . .

I cry the cruel cuts of Fate
   with eyes worn red from weeping,
whose fickle favours travel straight
   back into her keeping:
as ye read, so shall ye find –
   luck comes curly-headed
from the front, but round behind
   not a hair is threaded!

Dame Fortune once invited me
   to enjoy her blessing:
to riches' throne exalted me
   caring and caressing:
but from maximum renown,
   garlanded and fêted,
Fate stepped up and threw me down –
   glory dissipated!

Fortune's wheel goes round and round,
   down go all my talents:
others rising from the ground
   fly too high to balance:
so beware Fate's old routine,
   kings and lords and ladies –
for beneath her throne lies Queen
   Hecuba in Hades.

CB 17   Fickle Fortune

O Fortuna   velut luna
statu variabilis . . .

O how Fortune,
  inopportune,
apes the moon's inconstancy:
  waxing, waning,
  losing, gaining . . .
Life treats us detestably:
  first oppressing,
  then caressing,
shifts us like pawns in her play:
  destitution,
  restitution,
mixes and melts them away.

Fate — as vicious
  as capricious —
whirling your merry-go-round:
  evil doings,
  worthless wooings
crumble away to the ground:
  darkly stealing,
  unrevealing,
working against me you go:
  for your measure
  of foul pleasure
I bare my back to your blow.

Noble actions,
  fair transactions,
no longer fall to my lot:
  powers to make me
  and then break me

all play their part in your plot:
   now seize your time –
   waste no more time,
pluck these poor strings, then let go:
   since the strongest
   fall the longest
let the world share in my woe!

CB 19   A Begging Song

*Fas et nefas ambulant
pene passu pari . . .*

Good and Evil, going round
   arm-in-arm, advise us:
show how scattergoods compound
   the misdeeds of misers:
show how virtue is defined
   by its moderation –
     knife-edged in between
rival sins, requires a keen
   eye's discrimination.

Do you recall having read
   Cato's wise researches –
titled *Ethics* – where he said:
   'Cultivate the virtuous'?
This means: having set your heart
   on the joy of giving,
     give, first, careful thought
as to which men are the sort
   worthiest of receiving.

Whether with a cheery face
   or a kind reception
favour all with equal grace –
   but with one exception:
if you really seek renown
   don't just be a friend to
     any old riff-raff:
learn to sort the wheat from chaff –
   whom to help, and when to.

Giving just because you should,
   or from predilection,
is but relatively good –
   not perfect perfection.
Favouring the virtuous
   ups your reputation:
     so, to banish doubt,
get to know me inside out –
   then make your donation!

If you wisely winnow grain
   with the finest sieving,
fame will be your harvest gain –
   but beware, in giving,
not to pour the oil of your
   kindness on caprices:
     thus I praise – I who
so outCodrus Codrus – you
   who outCroesus Croesus!

CB 20   The Golden Mean

Est modus in verbis: duo sunt contraria verba . . .

I
Words lie in equipoise. Two,
  opposed, are worthy of mention:
GIVE is the first. With TAKE
  it's locked in endless contention.
GIVE, so the donor hopes,
  may earn him love for his labour –
But TAKE may assist the mean
  to be thought poor by his neighbour.

II
Always avoid extremes
  whatever your doings and schemes:
Where there's no balance at all
  governments go to the wall.

III
Virtue lies at a point midway be-
  tween two opposite vices:
Misdeeds mingle with good deeds –
  but so closely entangled
That virtue itself is all
  too often taken for vice.

IV
Fools, in avoiding one vice, run
  slap-bang into another.
Why? Because vice deceives
  by disguising itself as a virtue.

CB24   This World Rages

Iste mundus   furibundus   falsa prestet gaudia,
Quia fluunt   et decurrunt   ceu campi lilia . . .

This world rages   and presages
   dead-sea fruits for all its yield –
Which, once growing,   fall to mowing
   like the lilies of the field.
Proud position,   vain ambition
   lead us to our just reward:
Onward urge us   to submerge us
   down beneath the Stygian horde.
All our wheelings,   all our dealings,
   truly transitory, must
Crack and crumble,   totter, tumble
   into unsubstantial dust.
All we strive for,   stay alive for
   in our earthly entity
Will be shattered   lost and scattered
   like old leaves blown from the tree.
Let us therefore   cease to care for
   worldly joys, and turn them down –
Lest in sorrow   we tomorrow
   be denied our heavenly crown:
Let us bend to   put an end to
   corporal cupidity –
That among the   blessed number
   saved for immortality
We may merit   and inherit
   life through all eternity.

AMEN

CB 28   Ten Proverbs

Laudat rite Deum   qui vere diligit illum.

I   Who love the Lord   leave not His praise ignored.

II   They earn bright wings   who spurn all fleshly things.

III   What charms you most   for certain harms you most.

IV   If conscience guide   temptation's well defied.

V   Spare not your skin   to save a soul from sin.

VI   It is absurd   to go down with the herd.

VII   What's right and just   deserves our only trust.

VIII Such lips as lie   would see their owner die.

IX   The goodly life   shrinks not from mental strife.

X   A sin a day?   Then pray without delay!

CB 30   A New Leaf

Dum iuventus floruit,
licuit et libuit . . .

In my youth, when springtime teased
'twas as licit as it pleased
to trail as the fancy seized
    down the lanes of leisure:
to pursue   and follow through
    every earthly pleasure.

Ah! To live in such a way –
free of care, lead day to day
one long round of come what may –
   adulthood prevents us:
youth has cause   to quash the laws
   of custom and consensus.

Youth it was that did advise –
nay, that brooked no compromise
but URGED with complaisant lies:
   'Nothing is forbidden!
all you see   was made to be
   enjoyed and overridden.'

Let me drop this vain pretence.
For my sins (if lapse of sense
counts as such) I'll recompense –
   will profess for ever
serious things   and for my sins
   atone with all endeavour.

CB51a   A Crusading Song

Imperator rex Grecorum
minas spernens paganorum . . .

Emperor Manuel Comnenus,
scorning pagans' golden *minas*,
formed a treasury to match theirs:
armed an army to despatch theirs.

   Ayos
  o theos athanathos,
  ysma sather yskyros!
  miserere kyrios:
  us thy servants save from loss!

Amalrich, brave king and splendid –
from our northern race descended –
burst through Egypt's mighty portals,
smote the Turks and proved them mortals!

    Ayos
  o theos athanathos,
  ysma sather yskyros!
  miserere kyrios:
  us thy servants save from loss!

Christians all of rank and station,
Egypt earns your obligation:
smite her king with firm endeavour:
see her safe and sound for ever!

    Ayos
  o theos athanathos,
  ysma sather yskyros!
  miserere kyrios:
  us thy servants save from loss!

CB54   Incantation

Omne genus demoniorum,
cecorum,   claudorum,
sive confusorum . . .

Every kind of demon being –
  come hobbling,
  come squabbling,
sightless or unseeing –
mark well my words, my invocation,
my command, my incantation.

Creatures all of phantom company
who populate the principality
  of that vile dragon creeping
  with venom seeping –
whose high and mighty fundament
sweeps full one third the stars' extent –
  Gordan, Ingordin and Ingordan:
by the Seal of Solomon,
magi the Pharaohs call upon,
    I now exorcize you
    and substantialize you:
by sages three: Caspar,
Melchior and Balthazar:
    by David's playing
    for the allaying
    of Saul's dismaying
    and your gainsaying.

    I adjure you
    and conjure you
by the mandate of the Lord:
    be unkind not,
    hurt mankind not,
manifest misericord:
    show but once your faces
    and retract your traces
    with forsaken races
    to hell's hiding places.

    I adjure
    I conjure
  by that awesome
  by that fearsome
that gruesome Judgement Day,
    when unending punishment
and horror and dismay

and unbounded banishment
shall drive demonkind
   into damnation
but shrive humankind
   unto salvation.

By that same unnamed, unsaid,
that unutterably dread
   tetragrammaton of God:
fall to fear and trembling
as to disassembling
   I now exorcize
      spectres: demons: ghosts: hobgoblins:
      satyrs: sirens: hamadryads:
      nightmares: incubi and
      shades of the departed –
flee to ruination,
chaos and damnation,
lest your foul conflation
rend Christ's congregation.

From all our enemies, good Lord, deliver us.

II
Love and Nature

CB 62   Nocturne

Dum Diane vitrea
sero lampas oritur . . .

When Diana's crystalline
lantern rises late at night,
shimmering with undershine
from her brother's rosy light:
when the gentle Zephyr's breeze
whiffles little clouds with ease
    up and away . . .
    so then the lay
of lutenists and ligatures
    lures returning
    hearts from yearning
after lovers' overtures.

Hesperus with starlight beams
    drawing dewdrops,
    soothing dewdrops,
dulls with soporific dreams
mortal creatures and regimes.

    O how welcome, slumber! – sleep, the antidote
to all our inmost storms of hurt and doubt
    instils between the lids of eyes half shut
such ecstasy as ever love gave out.

Morpheus unminds us:
   weaving dreams, unwinds us
gentle winds from fields of ripening corn:
trickling streamlets over sandbeds borne:
an endless round and round of millwheels turning
robs our sleep-dimmed eyes of all discerning.

After exquisite toil at love's behest
the wearied brain sinks welcomely to rest:
eyes rediscover peace in growing dim,
yield in their raft of lids to sink or swim.
To pass from love to languor – yes, this is a sweet remove! –
but sweeter still the swift return to love.

From flesh fulfilled, contented perfumes spread
through all three layers of the lover's head,
   enveloping those selfsame eyes
   sleep strives to mesmerize:
over the eyelids draw their swirling shield
to hold the gaze from wandering far afield . . .
so do Nature's ministers soothe eyes into submission,
serving as the faithful guardians of our power of vision.

Under the shady greenwood tree
where the nightingale sings plaintively
   sweet to be lying there . . .
   sweeter, be trying there
      the playful whirl
      of a lovely girl
         in the grass:
and where the vagrant
scents of fragrant
      herbs have strayed
      and roses made
         a couching place . . .
there then the soft sustenance of sleep,
when lovers' toils are done, is happily relinquished
   to those by labour vanquished.

Oh what commotions
and variable devotions
agitate the heart's emotions!
how like an unanchored boat
on seas we float, we
fluctuate between hope and misgiving –
who champion Venus for a living.

CB66   The Steeds of Apollo

Acteon, Lampos,   Erythreus et Philogeus:
Istis nominibus   poterit spectare peritus . . .

Actaeon, Lampos, Erythreus and Philogaeus:
these names, to the expert, divide all the hours of the day
into four parts exactly: one name holds each part in its sway.

Actaeon first, being known to the Greeks as 'the Red',
reflects on the hue of the sun as he springs from his bed:

Next in succession, bright Lampos – nicknamed 'the
    Resplendent' –
rides on the sun as he rises upon the ascendant:

'Ardent Erychtheus' follows – that great ball of fire
we feel when the heat of the sun cannot rise any higher.

At last, Philogaeus, or 'Lover of Earth', takes his place –
so called because evening inclines him towards her embrace,
and his greatest wish is to grant her the blessing of peace.

CB 70   Summer Love

Estatis florigero tempore
sub umbrosa residens arbore . . .

Once upon a flowery summertime,
   stretched beneath a canopy of trees —
birdsong rang the woods around with rhyme
   to whispers hinting of an evening breeze —
I indulged with dearest Thisbe
   in delightful colloquy
turning on our views of Venus
   trafficking in ecstasy.

   In her face
     and grace
       and bearing
   she was far
     beyond
       comparing
as the sun
   outshines
     the stars:
   oh, how to cause
our sweet philosophy
to lead her favour me
with love's familiarity? . . .

. . . To make a full and frank confession
seems the wisest way to deal
with so repressed a passion.
May Fortune favour all who favour her designs!
   So I begin along these lines:

HE
Long and long a time I've nurtured
    secret fires within my breast! —
now they overwhelm my tortured
    frame, and I am all possessed:
you alone, would you but deign
    to see them, could put out their flame
happy I'd half live again
    bound as vassal to your name.

SHE
The heart's desire is so complex —
one moment true, and false the next —
that love's most urgent quality,
most requisite, is constancy.

Yes, other virtues play some part —
    like silent suffering,
that gentle handmaid of the heart . . .

But if it's flames that leap about
    within your breast — no doubt
some other flame can put them out!

Our love's not furtive or impure:
    we must try to ensure
its innocent delights endure.

HE
    The flames by which I die —
    yet which I glorify —
remain invisible to men:

    save she extinguish it
    by whom their fire was lit
never will it sink again.

Thus, yours is the command to give –
to sentence death – or let me live.

SHE
Why should I hazard life and limb
on so precarious a whim?

   My father, my mother –
   not to mention my brother –
go on at me about you day and night:

   they keep a careful eye on us
   by setting crones to spy on us
and boys at windows gawping for a sight!

Sticks and stones compare as trifles
to Argus and his hundred eyefuls.

   A man of honour
   would deem it proper
   to speak discreetly
   and so completely
protect his girl-friend's name from idle gossip.

HE
   Fear nothing, dearest,
   no one comes near us:
   Vulcan's the merest
buffoon, for all his complicated netting;
   mimicking Mercury's
   methods, I'll mesmerize
   Argus's hundred eyes –
drown them in the dew of sleep's forgetting.

SHE
Of the mind's frail balance one may see
   opposites claim mastery:
wanton desire vies with maidenly modesty.

I favour as I see, and so
　　meekly to the yoke I go.
But it's the sweetest yoke of all I know . . .

HE
What silly things you say!
That 'yoke' of Venus, in its way,
　　is freer than the air:
none gentler are nor worthier.

　　Darling are the heights
　　of Venus's delights
and her indiscretions holy.

　　Come then – why delay
　　to hear her and obey?
What's a gift worth, given slowly?

SHE
　　My dearest love –
Now I give you all I have . . .

CB 72   Thanks Be to Venus

Grates ago Veneri
　que prosperi . . .

　　　　Thanks to Lady Venus! She
　　　　　has granted me
　　　　one famous victory:
　　　　　charitably
　　　　induced my girl
　　　　to yield the pearl
　　　　　of her virginity!

A while ago this tough campaign
    seemed waged in vain:
unwaged went all my zeal –
    yet now I feel
supremely blessed
to have possessed
    Dione's company.

    A cuddle and a kiss,
    a glance, a hint of bliss,
my darling freely entertained –
    but still restrained
love's more complete design –
    that further line
        of rapture
which I had made a bond
    to pass beyond
to prizes that desire
    made me aspire
        to capture.

So I pursue that prize.
She, supplicant with sighs,
appeals, alluring in her straits:
    yet hesitates
whether or not to overhaul
    her last-to-fall
        defences.
Sweet-tasting tears! I drink them all:
    the more they fall
in vain endeavour to assuage,
    the fiercer rage
        my senses.

Flushed falls every little kiss
   with the waste of weeping eyes
which the blandishments of bliss
   only serve to emphasize:
so rekindling all desire
   my flames aspire
to consummate this loving:
but she, with the bitterness
   of Coronis,
tumbles headlong into tears
   and all my prayers
      gain nothing.

Plea on plea I aggregate,
   supplement with kiss on kiss:
neither will her tears abate,
   nor yet is she moved by this.
See: there sparks within her gaze
   no less a blaze –
soon, all too soon, receding;
now she struggles to break free –
   now clings to me –
but the more I press with prayers
   the less she bears
      my pleading.

Boldly I press home the advance.
Unsheathing her talons, she implants
   them in my hair,
   struggles to tear
away from me,
   now bends herself,
   defends herself,
knee over knee,
denying me
   the gate to her affections.

Then — (sound of trumpet! roll of drums!) —
triumphantly the breakthrough comes:
  with arms entwined
  I firmly bind
us tighter:
  with kisses pressed
  upon each breast
delight her:
excite her taste with
  intimate confections . . .

Both sides content with the affair,
she stopped protesting: couldn't bear
a lasting grudge — instead she bore
  me kisses, more
    and sweeter:

She smiled at me through half-closed eyes
with trembling lids, while troubled sighs
escaped her lips, as she grew tired
  and dreams conspired
    to cheat her.

CB75   Down with Study!

Omittamus studia
dulce est desipere . . .

Down with study! Books away!
  Come and learn a sweeter truth
finding pleasure in the play
  and the greenery of youth:
it's the pride of old professors
  to engage in serious things
and the joy of youth (God bless us!)
  to prefer venereous things.

> *Days go tumbling headlong by,*
>   *gone to waste on learning:*
> *young-at-heart were made to ply*
>   *trades of less discerning.*

Springtime slyly slithers by
   while our winter urges haste:
melancholies multiply,
   bits of body go to waste:
blood runs thin: the heart distresses:
   happinesses fade away:
age's brood of ills depress us
   by their odour of decay.

> *Days go tumbling headlong by,*
>   *gone to waste on learning:*
> *young-at-heart were made to ply*
>   *trades of less discerning.*

Let's be like those gods of yore —
   admirable sentiments! —
take our snares a-hunting for
   love in all its innocence:
mindful that the inmost urgings
   of our hearts are sure and sound,
come down to the street where virgins
   gather for their dancing round.

> *Days go tumbling headlong by,*
>   *gone to waste on learning:*
> *young-at-heart were made to ply*
>   *trades of less discerning.*

Oh what sights are for the seeing!
  Oh how palpable they seem!
Arms and legs go flashing free in
  time to music's merry scheme:
watching limbs evolve amazing
  patterns in that lithe display
I can only stand there gazing
  till my heart is plucked away.

Days go tumbling headlong by,
  gone to waste on learning:
young-at-heart were made to ply
  trades of less discerning.

CB77   The Dream of the Rose

Si linguis angelicis   loquar et humanis
non valeret exprimi   palma nec inanis . . .

1
Though I speak with tongues of men
  and angels — words must fail me
to do justice to the palm
  selected to regale me:
one that has exalted me
  throughout all generations —
even roused some critics to
  profane disapprobations.

2

O for a thousand tongues to sing
   its great redeeming praises!
But I'll leave the lady's name
   unmentioned: for the basis
of successful wooing is
   that one should always cover
with a cloak of secrecy
   the identity of one's lover.

3

Into a formal garden once
   I found myself resorting,
turning over in my mind
   the problem of a courting.
Do I sow on stony ground?
   My resolution wavers —
pining for the fairest rose,
   despairing of her favours.

4

Yet — if I despair, don't dare
   to count yourself astonished:
some old hellcat holds my Rose
   prevented and premonished
from feeling love herself, or finding
   love extended to her.
Pluto, rise and zap that crone!
   Get rid of her! Undo her!

5

Pondering upon my plight
   with more than warmth of feeling —
hoping that some thunderbolt
   might knock the old girl reeling —

Lo! Before I took my leave
   I turned, and saw behind me
that which fixed me to the spot:
   a vision fit to blind me.

6

There I saw the Flower of Flowers,
   I saw of flowers the fairest:
saw the early Rose of May –
   of roses all, the rarest:
saw, of all the stars in heav'n
   that coruscate, the clearest:
fell head over heels in love
   with her I held the dearest.

7

Seeing thus the object of
   so many years' adoring,
my heart leapt up: to heaven's door
   I found my spirit soaring.
So I rose and hastened to
   her side with footsteps fleeting,
there to humbly bend the knee
   and offer her this greeting.

8

'Hail to thee, thou priceless gem,
   perfect and resplendent:
hail, thou pride of maidenhood,
   virgin most transcendent:
hail, thou Rose of all the world,
   Light, all lights abasing:
Blanchefleur and Helen, thou,
   and Venus all-embracing.'

9

To which my Morning Star replied
   (for so I designate her):
'May the author of the earth
   and heaven's sole creator –
who studs the grass with violets
   and makes the roses prickly –
grant you fame and fortune, sir,
   and balsams when you're sickly!'

10

'Dearest darling!' I replied,
   'I hear my heart assure me
that of all the pains I bear
   you alone can cure me:
for the saying goes (and who
   am I to disbelieve it?)
"Whosoever strikes the blow
   can alone relieve it".'

11

'Do you mean to tell me, sir,
   you see in *me* the nameless
dealer of these mortal wounds?
   I'll have you know I'm blameless!
Still, if you would like to bare
   your wounds to diagnosis
maybe they're amenable
   to humble little doses.'

12

'What's the point of baring wounds'
   (I said) 'quite plainly showing?
Five full summers have gone by –
   now the sixth is going –

since that festive holiday
   when I first saw you dancing.
What a vision! Of them all
   you were the most entrancing.

13

'Seeing you, I found myself
   to this belief adhering:
"There's a virgin worthiest
   of anyone's revering!
Beautiful? She outdoes every-
   one by the perfection
of her form and figure, of
   her face and sweet complexion."

14

'What a face! – as shining fair
   and cool and captivating
as the sunshine-brimming air
   is sweetly scintillating;
I was so moved as to cry
   to Him the angels choir to:
"Is this Helen I adore –
   or Venus I aspire to?"

15

'How the tresses of your hair
   ran down like golden fountains
over shoulders white and fair
   as snow upon the mountains!
over breasts – O graceful pair
   of curves! How all suffices
to suggest a fragrance far
   beyond the rarest spices!

16

'From the twinkle of your eye
    the stars came bright and beaming:
in the sparkle of your teeth
    fine ivories lay gleaming:
such equilibrium of limbs
    I can't describe discreetly –
was there anyone you'd fail
    to captivate completely?

17

'Thus the links of all your looks
    unbreakably enchained me –
neither liberty of thought
    nor heart nor soul remained me:
henceforth to converse with you
    became my sole ambition:
alas – for years I found this goal
    frustrated of fruition.

18

'See the cause of my complaint,
    my source of disaffection –
life has treated me with more
    than my share of dejection:
who in any age or clime
    has been so harshly spited
as to find his warmest hopes
    so coldly unrequited?

19

'This, then, is the bolt I've borne,
    deep in the body lying,
whence a thousand times and more
    I supplicate with sighing,

saying "Founder of all things –
    what trespass have I done Thee
that the loads of all who ever
    loved are lumped upon me?"

20

'I have lost my appetite:
    slumber fails to lure me:
I can find no medicine
    to call upon to cure me.
Lord: from such fine sufferings
    suffer me no sunder –
help me undergo them all
    without going under!

21

'Prey to all these buffetings –
    and more beside – I languish,
void of aught to mitigate
    unmitigable anguish –
save that many a time and oft
    in dead of night's duration
I have lain alone with you –
    in my imagination.

22

'Rose! Now that you see how deep
    the wounds are I complain of –
know the tortures you inflict
    that I have cried in vain of –
only say the words, I beg,
    that prove you won't deny me:
make me well again: restore
    my health: revivify me!

23

'Say yes – and I shall redound
  to your glorification:
cedars none of Lebanon
  shall match my exaltation.
If (and this I can't believe)
  you offer me no prospect
then I'm cast upon the rocks
  and die forever shipwrecked.'

24

Radiantly, my Rose replied:
  'The tortures you have been through
inwardly are known to me
  and so more clearly seen through:
what I've borne on *your* behalf
  would pass your comprehension:
for I've suffered twice as much
  from any pain you mention.

25

'But I mustn't bore you with
  the cares of my recital –
wishing, as I rather would,
  to offer some requital:
something to restore your health,
  to leave you well and sunny –
something in the nature of
  a sweeter balm than honey.

26

'Tell me therefore, gentle youth,
  exactly what your itch is:
is it silver you require,
  and other sorts of riches?

Or is it decorative gems
    you'd rather lay a claim to?
If I can, I'll grant you all
    you care to put a name to.'

27

'No, they're *not* my heart's desire!
    Riches fail to woo me:
What I need is more than wealth
    and more important to me –
that which makes the impossible
    the simplest of achievement
and overrides with sweet delights
    the dolours of bereavement.'

28

'What you long for then, I fear
    defies my comprehension –
yet, to grant your heart's desire
    remains my firm intention:
therefore come to me – what's mine
    is yours but for the taking:
seek, that you may find in me
    some balm to soothe your aching.'

29

Say no more! I threw my arms
    around her neck, and pressing
countless kisses to her lips
    received a like redressing:
and a million million times
    I listened to me crying
'Surely, this is that relief
    for which my heart was dying!'

30

Who'll pretend to ignorance
   of all that followed after?
Sighs and sorrows passed away,
   dissolved in lovers' laughter:
paradisal ecstasies
   were magnified within us
and the sweetest of delights
   administered to twin us.

31

So a hundredfold we reaped
   the harvest of our pleasure:
so in mistress and in me
   joy multiplied in measure:
so I am rewarded with
   that palm, the prize of lovers —
so I now declare my name
   blessed above all others.

32

You who know the hurt of love,
   hark to one who knew it:
bear such heartbreak as you must
   without succumbing to it:
be assured, there's bound to dawn
   a day of compensation
when the glory of your pain
   shall find its consummation.

33

Out of wildernesses rise
    proud pinnacles of pleasure:
out of trials and tribulations
    everlasting treasure:
all who ride in quest of honey,
    when to gall submitted –
be prepared for better things
    the more you are embittered!

CB85   Julie by the Greenwood Tree

Veris dulcis in tempore
florenti stat sub arbore
Iuliana cum sorore . . .

In serenest spring you'll see
Julie by the greenwood tree
in her sister's company –
    Dulcis amor!
who pass you by when spring is nigh
    care nothing for!

Now that trees are blossoming
birds lasciviously sing,
maidens' dreams are on the wing –
    Dulcis amor!
who pass you by when spring is nigh
    care nothing for!

Now that lilies bloom again
to the gods in heavenly train
girls direct their hearts' refrain —
   Dulcis amor!
who pass you by when spring is nigh
   care nothing for!

Could I clasp whom I adore
on the forest's leafy floor,
how I'd kiss her — Oh and more!
   Dulcis amor!
who pass you by when spring is nigh
   care nothing for!

CB 87 Love Rules Everything

Amor tenet omnia,
mutat cordis intima . . .

Love rules everything — controls
all the movement of our souls
to its preappointed goals:
vies with honey-sweetness, yes —
and with gall in bitterness.
   Blindly chaste, Love
does away with modesty:
freezingly and boilingly
   and tepidly
Love's courageous, cowardly,
and faithless in fidelity.

Now's the time: the season's fine:
Love bids lovers all entwine
and the birds in song combine.
Love holds young men in its sway,
wills young women to its way . . .
    Push off, Old Age –
you pollute the atmosphere!
Fiche-moi! I have my dear,
    sweet Theoclea
whom I love most and revere.
Age! As a pest you have no peer.

Whether love play false or true
doesn't mean a fig to you:
killing time is all you do,
nodding miseries away –
nothing's worse than Age, I say.
    Venus keeps us
young and fresh with happiness:
worthy that togetherness
    which I so bless –
be it free of your duress!
What finer joys could one profess?

Cupid hovers in the air
loosing darts off everywhere:
every belle desires to pair
with a beau to suit herself –
none must be left on the shelf:
    otherwise she
makes herself a mockery:
binds herself by lock and key
    in custody
of nightlong profundity . . .
How harsh her fate, her misery!

Love's naïve, but leads you on:
ruddy-cheeked, but pale and wan:
first deranges everyone
then proves meek and pliable –
firmly unreliable.
   Cupid, though,
can be controlled himself, with care:
find a bed – he couldn't bear
   to be elsewhere
when the night is soft and rare . . .
Love catches easy in that snare!

CB 90   Rosebud

Exiit diluculo   rustica puella
cum grege, cum baculo,   cum lana novella . . .

A rustical rosebud
   arose with the sun,
took flock and took crook
   and some wool to be spun.

Her little flock boasted
   a sheep and a she-goat,
a heifer, a bullock,
   an ass and a he-goat.

She spotted a scholar
   ensconced by a tree:
'What are you doing, sir? –
   Come and do me!'

CB 92   All about Phyllis and Flora

Anni parte florida,   celo puriore,
picto terre gremio   vario colore,
dum fugaret sidera   nuntius Aurore,
liquit somnus oculos   Phyllidis et Flore . . .

1

It was the flowery time of year —
    the sky was never purer:
Mother Earth was all arrayed
    in colourful bravura:
stars were being swept away
    by order of Aurora —
when sleep arose and fled the eyes
    of Phyllis and of Flora.

2

Waking to a rather more
    than melancholy feeling,
both declared the prospect of
    a morning ride appealing:
so they set off side by side
    in search of somewhere pleasing
till they found a meadow made
    for idling and heart's easing.

3

Picture them: two pretty maids
    of noble line descended —
Phyllis with her flowing hair,
    Flora's coiffed and tended:
more like goddesses than girls,
    they needed no adorning
as they sparkled to the sunshine
    of a lovely morning.

4

You'd know they were not commoners
    from breeding, looks and grooming,
and in their ways, as in their years,
    the flower of youth was blooming.
Yet there was one respect in which
    they took dissenting stances:
one loved a CLERIC, while her friend
    preferred a KNIGHT's advances.

5

You'd find no other difference
    to judge by or divide them –
beauty twinned them, and two hearts
    beat as one inside them:
two of a kind, you would have said,
    by habit and by fashion –
except – and only – in the way
    each yielded to her passion.

6

Murmurs of a gentle breeze
    blew up from the meridian:
the place was gay with greenery
    from emerald to viridian:
somewhere, hidden in the grass,
    a little stream went splashing,
chatting merrily to itself,
    now dithering, now dashing.

7

Embellishing this lovely scene,
    and offering some protection,
a pine tree stood beside the stream –
    a model of perfection:

its sweeping branches circumscribed
   a cooling reservation
guarding them against the sun's
   unauthorized invasion.

8

Happy with this grassy spot
   the girls reclined upon it,
Phyllis by the little stream,
   Flora further from it.
As they sat, to catch their breath
   and soothe their ankles' aching,
they were assailed by pangs of love,
   as though their hearts were breaking.

9

And so they were. For in them both
   love lay repressed but throbbing –
welled up in their heaving hearts
   and set them both to sobbing:
a pallor settled on their cheeks
   that drained them of expression –
but neither of them felt inclined
   to give way to confession.

10

Phyllis heard a sighing sound
   that seemed to come from Flora –
but Flora had, contrariwise,
   heard Phyllis sigh before her:
each having caught the other out,
   there seemed no point in hiding –
so, established face to face,
   they set about confiding.

11

The subject they embark upon
  in their unhurried fashion
leads into a long debate
  on love's exquisite passion:
love it is that fills their hearts
  and shines forth from their faces . . .
smiling at Flora, Phyllis first
  explains her own love's basis.

*

12

'Dearest Paris!' (she began)
  'sweet knight in shining armour:
where are you campaigning now,
  where dying in some drama?
Oh, the military life
  evokes such grand emotions:
no career is worthier
  of Venus's devotions!'

13

As she extolled her gallant beau
  with amorous confessions,
Flora grinned and rolled her eyes
  and practised pained expressions:
after that she giggled, and
  remarked – somewhat unkindly –
'You might as well declare you love
  a ragamuffin blindly!

14

'Ah – but Alcibiades:
  where are *you*, my dearest? –
who of all the race of men
  are noblest and sincerest? –

who by Nature has been blessed
    with grace beyond all measure?
none can match your sweet rewards,
    the cleric's highest pleasure.'

15
Phyllis, finding Flora's speech
    a shade too braggadocian,
gave her companion tit for tat,
    her voice strained with emotion:
'Hark at you! A baby doll
    whose heart so innocently
goes out to an epicure
    and hopes he'll treat it gently!

16
'Give up, give up, you silly girl
    this odious obsession!
Mark my words – the cleric's is
    a hedonist's profession:
lacking all refinement, he
    belies your adulation,
trapped inside his gross display
    of self-gratification.

17
'Cupid's treasures never were
    entrusted to the keeping
of one whose heart is given up
    to food and drink and sleeping:
nice girls like yourself should know
    what everyone confesses:
how each knight has made a vow
    to hold from such excesses.

18

'The knight has always been content
  to live on bare essentials,
seeking neither bed nor food
  nor drink on his credentials:
love prevents his giving way
  to idle somnolescence:
for sustenance he takes romance
  and youthful effervescence.

19

'Who'd compare *your* boy-friend to
  my own love, for a second?
By what common qualities
  can both be fairly reckoned?
Mine excels at making love –
  yours in merry-making:
mine devotes his energies
  to giving – yours, to taking.'

20

Flora's modest face grew pale
  as anger overtook her:
then she gave a lovely smile
  once more, as ire forsook her:
for an argument had sprung
  to mind – a notion subtle,
prompting her to undertake
  an eloquent rebuttal:

21

'Phyllis dear' (her friend began)
  'how cleverly you put it!
Your eloquence is finely honed,
  your train of thought sure-footed.

The trouble is, it isn't true!
　　It makes you sound so silly –
as if you really do prefer
　　the hemlock to the lily!

22

'A life of luxury you deem
　　to be the cleric's choosing:
a slave, you claim, to idleness,
　　to banqueting and boozing!
Slander is the very sound
　　of vice describing virtue –
now it's my turn! Here's a thought
　　I think may disconcert you.

23

'I'll admit my boy-friend makes
　　a reasonable living –
but you can't accuse him of
　　achieving it by thieving,
for he earns his share of corn
　　and oil, of wine and honey,
goblets of gold, and precious stones
　　worth not a little money.

24

'Added to the sweet rewards
　　of cleric's benefices –
sweeter than can be described
　　by verbal artifices –
Cupid blesses him with wings
　　that beat the air, extending
indefatigable love,
　　immortal and unending.

25

'Cupid's darts sink just as deep
　　into the cleric's passions —
and since he cannot be accused
　　of going short of rations,
or sticking out all skin and bone
　　from indigence and fasting,
so the love his mistress bears
　　must be everlasting.

26

'But what a pale and paltry thing
　　you've picked on for *your* pining!
Sir Penniless of purse unlined
　　and cloak without a lining:
neither strength, nor strength of mind,
　　enhance his constitution,
and when he has no wars to fight
　　he lacks all resolution.

27

'It's disgraceful to admire
　　a man who lacks a living!
What's a knight to offer when
　　his honour calls for giving?
Clerics give the more away
　　the more their income waxes:
they who earn a lot must pay
　　a large amount of taxes.'

28

Phyllis, interrupting, said:
　　'You're clearly well acquainted
with the facts of one, and how
　　the other has been painted —

hence the decorative lies
    embroidering your chatter!
Don't think for a moment, though,
    that this concludes the matter.

29
'When a feast or holy-day
    attends the true believer,
then your dreary friend appears –
    that consummate deceiver! –
black as sin from head to foot
    and shaven by profession,
patently the worse for wear
    beneath his pi expression.

30
'Who can be so ignorant,
    so blind by predilection,
as to fail to recognize
    in knighthood man's perfection?
Your friend grows with idleness –
    so sheep and cows grow larger!
My friend bears a helmet and
    is borne upon a charger.

31
'Mine rides through the enemy
    to scatter their positions:
yet, although he may alight
    for single combat missions –
leaving bold Bucephalus
    to Ganymede's assuaging –
still he thinks of whom he loves
    amidst the battle's raging!

32

'Home returning from the fight,
  the enemy defeated,
visor raised, he seeks my sight –
  for I must be first greeted!
These and countless other grounds
  of right and obligation
show why chivalry commands
  my utmost admiration.'

33

Flora, seeing Phyllis heave,
  how warm her indignation,
gave as good as she had got
  with grim determination.
'You sit there like a mutton-head
  and to the wind you wheedle –
trying to pass a camel through
  the eyehole of a needle!

34

'You can't distinguish honeycomb
  from wormwood, truth from lying,
if it's armour you approve,
  the cloth you're vilifying.
Is it love that makes knights prey
  to wild, barbaric forces?
No, dear! It's their poverty,
  their absence of resources.

35

'Phyllis: lovely as you are,
  would that you loved more wisely –
and didn't contradict the truth
  so loudly and precisely!

Your soldier's constantly assailed
   by thirst and hunger's legions:
they alone will drag him down
   to Death's infernal regions.

36

'Misfortune grinds the soldier down
   with permanent oppression;
he's drawn the harshest lot of all –
   a perilous profession:
his life hangs daily by a thread –
   he has no way of knowing
whether he'll earn the crust of bread
   he needs to keep him going.

37

'You wouldn't mouth such obloquy
   if you were not so unsure
why a cleric wears the black
   and a distinctive tonsure:
they're a mark of worthiness:
   they're honour's indicators:
he wears them as a symbol of
   his higher social status.

38

'No one fails to recognize
   his right to be respected:
from his very crown one sees
   authority projected:
knights depend on him and heed
   his every requisition –
thus the master's role excels
   the menial's position.

39

'You'd see him convicted as
    a good-for-nothing neighbour.
I'll admit he doesn't soil
    his hands by common labour –
but whenever he can rest
    from cleric's obligations
he explores astronomy
    and Nature's revelations.

40

'My love wears a crimson robe –
    yours wears a thing of leather:
yours gets involved in silly fights –
    mine in the pillow's feather:
mine sits and reads of noble deeds
    from ancient recollections –
writes to, thinks of, dreams about
    the girl of his affections.

41

'As for Venus's delights
    and Cupid's gifts to lovers,
clerics were vouchsafed them first
    and then taught all the others:
knights can only know of love
    through clerical instruction.
Every word you say is proof
    of culpable traduction.'

42

Flora here ran out of steam
    and stopped the disputation:
Cupid, she declared, should be
    approached for arbitration.

'No!' said Phyllis first – then 'Yes'
  on subsequent revision.
Back they went across the fields,
  agreed on their decision.

43

Thus the final outcome turned
  on Cupid – both concurring
that his word was bound to be
  as expert as unerring:
he'd be versed in all the pros
  and cons of their opinions.
So the pair of them prepared
  to visit his dominions.

*

44

Equal in their courtliness
  and equal in their beauty,
each pursued her equal path
  with equal sense of duty –
Phyllis by mule, her friend by horse.
  And whereas Phyllis wore a
robe of white, a coloured dress
  had been the choice of Flora.

45

The mule that carried Phyllis was
  a marvel, no mistaking:
Neptune had been responsible
  for breeding it and breaking.
Aphrodite owned it first
  as gift of consolation
for Adonis's demise
  in hunting recreation.

46

She in turn presented it
  to Phyllis's late mother —
(a Spanish noblewoman, far
  more fair than any other) —
for her faithful services.
  Thereafter, by succession,
it passed into Phyllis's
  perpetual possession.

47

It proved the perfect complement
  to this young lady's nature:
handsome and intelligent,
  and of exquisite stature —
all, in short, you would expect
  of one that had been given
to a goddess by a god
  as far away as heaven.

48

Those who take more interest in
  the trappings than the bearer
will wish to know, a SILVER BIT
  constrained its happy wearer.
For the rest, suffice to say
  it was of such perfection
as befits a present of
  Neptunian selection.

49

As to beauty, at the same time,
  Phyllis earned no stricture:
she in all her finery
  looked pretty as a picture.

So her friend – comparison
   between the two were idle:
for of the most stupendous steed
   fair Flora held the bridle.

50

From pedigree of Pegasus
   he might have been descended –
so finely formed, no worldly price
   could well be recommended:
piebald in the purest sense –
   as though by painters tinted –
black upon the white of swan
   lay perfectly imprinted.

51

In the springtime of his life
   he handled well and truly:
with a lively sort of air –
   proud, but not unruly;
from lofty neck a silky mane
   in flowing stream descended:
shoulders well shaped: head compact,
   with delicate ears appended.

52

Upon his gently curving back
   the girl could settle neatly –
and she so light, all sense of weight
   eluded him completely:
hollow-hoofed, straight-lined at shin,
   stout-thighed – this noble creature
was from every point of view
   a masterpiece of Nature.

53

Athwart the mount a saddle-chair
   was laid, prepared and waiting,
consisting of a frame of gold
   infilled with ivory plating;
as the pommels of the chair
   were four, so each one ended
in a gem that sparkled like
   a star from heaven suspended.

54

It was cleverly engraved
   with many decorations
depicting ancient (not to say
   mysterious) visitations –
such as the marriage of Mercury
   with all the gods attendant –
the happy pair exchanging vows
   'midst wedding gifts resplendent.

55

You'd have a job to find a single
   spot void of incision –
it boasted more than anyone
   could possibly envision:
even Vulcan – who alone
   had carved it – on inspection
hardly could believe his hands
   the source of such perfection.

56

He had left Achilles' shield
   on one side, in suspension,
devoting to this work of art
   the whole of his attention

down to horseshoes, bridle, bit,
   and suchlike of that genus:
as for reins, he put to use
   the hair of his wife, Venus!

57

Its crimson-rich caparison
   was of Minerva's making:
she'd woven flax (her other work,
   pro tempore, forsaking),
embroidered it with flowers – to wit
   acanthus and narcissus –
and edged it with a scalloped fringe
   cut out with pinking scissors.

58

As the two young ladies put
   the creatures through their paces
intimate emotions bloomed
   upon their cheeks and faces:
so do roses bloom, and lilies
   from the ground emerging:
so twin stars roll heav'n around
   at one another's urging.

59

To the Paradise of Love
   they turned, their destination,
each displaying in her face
   such sweet determination;
each ribbed the other for her views
   with laughter of the shrillest.
A falcon rode with Flora, and
   a sparrowhawk with Phyllis.

*

60

Groves and pastures greeted them
    a little while thereafter,
and, just where the woods began,
    a flowing stream made laughter;
the air was redolent with myrrh,
    with balm the breeze abounding:
strains of harp and tambourine
    were delicately sounding.

61

Every sound the mind of man
    was capable of telling
took the maidens' breath away
    by its melodious swelling:
instruments of every kind
    made harmonies a-plenty —
both of diatessaron
    and of diapente.

62

From symphonies and psalteries
    sweet harmonies ascended:
voice of lyre and tambourine
    were beautifully blended:
tinkling cymbals, too, conjoined
    their tender treble with them —
while pipes of Pan were played upon
    to lithe and lilting rhythm.

63

Every bird you ever heard
    involved itself in voicing:
blackbirds dulcet and delightful
    joined in the rejoicing

with doves and larks – while Philomel,
   the nightingale, reflected
on the legendary pains
   to which she'd been subjected.

64

From the sounds of instruments
   and voices, and the singing –
from the rich variety
   of flowers around them springing –
from the perfumes and the scents
   that through the glades came gliding –
here, they felt, the God of Love
   was sure to be residing.

65

With some degree of diffidence
   they found themselves advancing,
but increasingly fell prey
   to amorous entrancing:
every little bird around
   sang each to its own calling
finding echo in their hearts
   to melodies enthralling.

66

One might grow immortal who
   remained here to be nourished,
where a tree for every fruit
   one could have wished for flourished:
where mint and thyme and lemon balm
   left pathways sweetly smelling . . .
thus the nature of the god
   is witnessed by his dwelling.

67

Dancing rings of boys and girls
    entranced the couple's vision,
each a heavenly body of
    perfection and precision.
Phyllis and Flora caught their breath,
    both wide-eyed with amazement:
such delights, undreamed-of sights,
    were quite beyond appraisement.

68

Halting, they with one accord
    dismounted – hardly bringing
thought to bear upon their strife,
    so soothing was the singing:
then they heard again the voice
    of Philomel complaining –
whereupon their ardour grew
    for amorous campaigning.

69

All around the middle of
    the wood a shrine lay hidden,
where devotees of the god
    to offices were bidden:
fauns, nymphs, satyrs crowded round
    in fulsome congregation,
sounding timbrels, and in song
    expressing adoration.

70

They sang with garlands and with cups
    of wine in their possession:
Bacchus choreographed the nymphs
    and led the fauns' procession:

all kept time and well in step
   with dance and music-making –
except Silenus – too far gone
   for such an undertaking.

71

Propped up on an ass, the drowsy
   gaffer trotted after –
making Bacchus fall about
   with uncontrollable laughter.
'Bring me wi –' the old man cried.
   his words but half completed:
thus do age and alcohol
   leave utterance defeated.

72

Cupid, son of Venus, now
   appeared amidst the teeming:
feathered wings sprang from his back,
   his face was bright and beaming:
he bore a bow in his left hand,
   a quiver at his shoulder,
evincing such divinity
   as might stun the beholder.

73

The sceptre of this cherub-god
   was intricate with flowers,
and perfume from his scented locks
   expired its fragrant powers.
Three Graces bore his chalice: they
   with fingers interlinking
made their reverence to him,
   each on one knee sinking.

74

Drawing near, the girls felt safe
    to join in adoration
of this god, whose youthful looks
    commanded veneration:
moved by majesty, they sensed
    a thrill of pride run through them
as he met their gaze, and made
    a friendly greeting to them.

75

He asked the reason for their ride,
    and, at their explanation,
praised them for initiative
    and proud determination.
'Make yourselves at home,' he smiled,
    'I'll offer a suggestion:
let's put this case before our court
    and *they*'ll decide the question.'

76

As he was a god, they knew
    there was no need to mention
all the points of their debate
    or detail their dissension:
so they led their animals
    to grass and satisfaction
while Cupid called upon his court
    to expedite their action.

77

Love has judges, Love has courts
    by which such things are reckoned:
Custom is the first of these
    and Nature is the second:

on them, questions of import
   soon find themselves depending,
for they see the future and
   the past in line unending.

78

Off to counselling they went
   and set about debating –
back they came with verdict from
   robust deliberating:
'By virtue of their learning and
   the customs they inherit –
we declare the love of CLERICS
   worthier of merit.'

79

All unanimously praised
   the judges' welcome finding,
claiming that from this day forth
   the verdict should be binding.
MORAL She who loves a knight,
   and trusts him with her honour,
be assured – a sorry plight
   is set to fall upon her!

CB95   Suspicion

Cur suspectum   me tenet domina?
Cur tam torva   sunt in me lumina?

Why does my lady eye me circumspectly –
with piercing glance, as though she would dissect me?
I swear by heaven, and may God's truth protect me,
I shun that vice of which she may suspect me.

Tort a vers mei ma dama!

The sky will flood to harvest corn and wine,
the air engender tangled elm and vine,
the sea throw game to huntsmen from the brine –
before the sins of Sodom count as mine.

Tort a vers mei ma dama!

If proudly prince bribed me with all his might
or penury should threaten with its blight –
I'd not be one of those who seek delight
in what's the done thing rather than the right.

Tort a vers mei ma dama!

I do enjoy pursuit of love's sweet goal –
but in the active, not the passive role:
I'd rather stay pure and go on the dole
than wind up wealthy with a filthy soul.

Tort a vers mei ma dama!

Thank God England always has been free
from this perversion, this obscenity!
I'd sooner die here than return to be
responsible for her depravity.

Tort a vers mei ma dama!

CB 111 Lovers' Grieving

O comes amoris, dolor,
cuius mala male solor,
  an habes remedium? . . .

Love's companion, lovers' grieving –
wretchedness beyond relieving –
  say, have you no remedy?
Grief impels me, little wonder,
into exile – cast asunder
  from one who outclasses me:
one whose singular perfection
might cause Paris's rejection
  of fair Helen's company.

Yet – why should I balk at being
far from her who looks, unseeing,
  down on my devotedness? –
whose name is so awe-inspiring
that I dare not, in admiring,
  say whose person I address? –
who, indeed, so often glances
through me as to prove my stance is
  nothing more than meaningless?

Let me go on being lonely:
hooked on her line, love her only:
  unrequited, adulate her . . .
There's a certain valley where she
dwells – a paradise I'll swear she
  makes it – where the good Creator
once saw fit to form this creature
pure in heart and fair of feature:
  from the depths I supplicate her.

O rejoice and sing for pleasure,
valley rich with roses' treasure,
      of all vales the loveliest:
most elect of valleys ever
graced by sun and moon together
      and by dulcet birdsong blessed –
vale by nightingale enchanted:
kindest vale that ever granted
      solace to the sore distressed.

CB114   Summer Yearning

Tempus accedit floridum,
      hiems discedit temere . . .

The season flowers adorn is here
      and winter's firmly on the wane,
and everything that once lay sere
      comes struggling into leaf again.
My lad, as down life's road you go,
be thankful if you never know
how cruelly love can lay you low!

How merrily the meadow beams!
      Of gathering garlands, who can tire?
But night descends – and, with it, dreams
      of unfulfillable desire.
What else, alas, is there to do
but, Lady Venus, turn to you?
Grant me the grace to see me through.

My grieving heart groans discontent
   for want of ultimate relief:
I know your generous consent
   is all I need to quell my grief.
Sweet virgin, loveliest of that breed:
if you should hear and yet not heed —
my death's the dismallest indeed!

Delectable you are to most
   yet most delectable to me:
there's no other girl to boast
   herself your peer in purity.
Consider me with kindliness,
to whom on your account accresce
sighs, sufferings, such sadnesses.

CB 116   Passions of Old

Sic mea fata canendo solor
ut nece proxima facit olor . . .

So do I sing as a comfort to care,
sing like a swan seeing death in the air:
sweet is the pain that I suffer and bear,
faded the colour my face used to wear:
   troubles increasing
   commitments unceasing
   and vigour decreasing
     I die of despair:
love, how it troubles and tries me — I swear
   I will die
   I will die
   I will die of despair —
forced into passions no partner will share!

Happy, more happy than Jove I should grow
　　could she I long for find love to bestow:
if at her lips I could feel the pulse flow –
one night, just one night to sleep with her – oh
　　gladly the dying
　　calmly the lying
　　death undefying
　　　I could undergo! –
did not such happiness first lay me low:
　　yes, undergo
　　undergo
　　undergo
were such a prize ever given to know.

How, when I gaze on that bosom undressed,
I could wish mine were the hands that caressed,
playfully fondled each virginal breast!
So do I daydream, by Venus possessed:
　　to see her afire
　　at the cheeks with desire –
　　and shame – I aspire
to her lips to be pressed:
　　her lips to be pressed
　　her lips to be pressed
　　her lips to be pressed –
and thrill to the making of love manifest.

CB 118   Love in Exile

Doleo quod nimium
patior exilium . . .

Grief is mine, for I am banned,
exiled to a foreign land –
university, be damned!
     Je m'en irai
if she's being underhand,
     ma désirée.

Of your face the loveliness
makes me weep, me weep *sans cesse*
that you have a heart of ice:
     pour remédier
you could bring me back to life
     par un baiser.

How shall I bear such dismay,
stuck in France? – A pointless stay
if the love has gone astray
     de la gentille.
Should I sadly run away
     from *ce pays?*

Quand viendrai à mon pays,
autre amant elle aura pris –
peu dura, laissa jadis:
     oh pity me,
for whom the *grand amour*
     means agony!

Be it night or be it day
in my timeless disarray,
hearing maidens *bavarder*
　　me fait complaindre:
and the more I sigh away
　　plus me sens craindre.

Comrades, for a *jeu d'esprit*
summon your philosophy
to dispel my misery:
　　grande douleur
bids you bend an ear to me –
　　pour votre honneur.

O *ma mie – c'est par ardeur*
that I suffer, *que je pleure:*
tous reconnaissent le coeur
　　brisé d'amour.
Friends, farewell: I'm off to her
　　sans perdre un jour!

CB 119　Dearest Homeland

Dulce solum　　natalis patrie
domus ioci,　　thalamus gratie . . .

Dearest homeland, where newborn once I lay –
happy cottage, where I was pleased to play –
I must leave you, tomorrow or today:
so love-shattered, I wait to pass away.

Farewell, world, and farewell to all thereon
from whose faces the light of friendship shone:
with whom schooldays were all too swiftly gone:
spare some weeping for one who passes on.

All-consuming love burns away my mind –
torture such as I never dreamt to find.
Now I see the old proverb underlined:
'If love is here, can tears be far behind?'

How many bees abound in Hybla's vales?
How many trees line Dodon's sacred pales?
How many fish ride round the ocean trails? –
So many sorrows lie where love prevails.

CB 126   Pity Me

Huc usque, me miseram!
rem bene celaveram . . .

Pity me in misery.
Though I loved clandestinely
   and bore my secret well

Now there's no disguising it –
I'm too far gone not to admit
   what every eye can tell.

Mother grinds me with her tongue.
Father rants at what I've done.
   Oh God, they give me hell.

I sit at home, all day, alone,
my features unfit to be shown.
   O friends, good times, farewell!

If I do dare venture out
folk flock to gape from miles about
   as if I were a freak.

Noting my rotundity
they wink and nudge as I pass by –
   but none of them will speak.

They prod with eloquent elbow;
their fingers point me out as though
   my status were unique.

With nods and winks they get across
my good-for-nothingness because
   I sinned once – oh, the cheek!

Have I left anything out?
I'm all they ever talk about –
   pride of their gossiping.

As if that weren't enough for me
My boy-friend has been forced to flee
   this tiny little thing.

Minding Dad's intemperance
he has removed himself to France –
   the furthest part away.

I miss him, miss him very much.
Death welcomes me, my grief is such.
   I weep all night, all day.

Parted from the one I love
how shall I ever rise above
   this depth of misery?

CB 129   Poor Scholar

Exul ego clericus
    ad laborem natus . . .

I, a scholar far from home,
    born of poor relations,
suffer every single day
    poverty's privations.

Literature and learning crave
    all of my endeavour –
only penury impels
    me from them to sever.

My poor cloak, so very thin,
    fails to keep the cold out:
drained of warmth, against the wind
    I can hardly hold out.

Even at church services
    I begin regressing
long before the closing hymn
    and the final blessing.

Venerable Lord (What's-his-name),
    you're a famed patrician:
won't you grant me something, pray,
    suiting your position?

May St Martin's deed inspire:
    bear in mind what he did:
draped upon a pilgrim's back
    something warmly needed.

So to heaven's kingdom may
    God Himself invite you,
and with beatific joys
    evermore requite you.

CB 130   Swan Song

Olim lacus colueram,
olim pulcher exstiteram,
dum cygnus ego fueram . . .

Once I had lakes to live upon:
in glory I would swim along –
once, when I was still a swan.

Poor thing, poor thing –
    not a raw thing
but done like anything!

Once I was whiter than the snow,
finer than any bird I know:
now see me – blacker than a crow!

Poor thing . . .

Cook on the spit is curving me,
flames sear through every nerve in me –
now here's a waiter *serving* me!

Poor thing . . .

I'd rather be in the fresh air
out on a lake – or anywhere
but peppered up as gourmet's fare.

   Poor thing . . .

Here in this serving dish I lie
where I have no strength to fly
as grinding molars greet the eye . . .

   Poor thing . . .

CB 136   Sunshine Rules

Omnia sol temperat
purus et subtilis . . .

Sunshine overrules the world
   peaceably and purely,
April with her veil unfurled
   bares herself demurely:
now to thoughts of love anew
   everyone confesses,
happily surrend'ring to
   Eros's caresses.

Spring inspiring once a year
   nature's new condition
bids us follow with good cheer
   in the old tradition:
may the springtime of your youth
   lead you to discover
how to stay in trust and truth
   faithful to your lover.

Therefore love me faithfully,
    mark my own devotion:
may it be whole-heartedly
    and with resolution.
I am with you everywhere
    far away though wending:
all who love like this must bear
    agonies unending.

CB 138   Spring Unveils Herself

Veris leta facies
mundo propinatur . . .

Spring unveils herself again,
    smiling on creation;
winter's rule of wind and rain
    falls in ruination;
gaily garlanded and crowned,
    Flora bids adherence;
birds rejoice and woods resound
    at her reappearance.

Phoebus with his sunny smile
    cleaves to Flora's breast –
both anew in flowery style
    colourfully dressed:
Zephyrus eke with sweet breath
    warmly wafts above us
while we strive, as to the death,
    for the prize of lovers.

Pretty maids with one accord
  call on men of letters,
meriting the common horde
  far beneath their betters.
Love draws everyone along,
  willingly entwining:
Venus sharing in their throng
  and the summer shining.

Charmingly the nightingale
  whiles away the hours,
meadows merrily regale
  all the world with flowers:
from the woods the bird-flock whirls
  a myriad of flights —
while a ring of dancing girls
  hints of greater heights.

CB 143   Welcome Season

Ecce gratum   et optatum
  ver reducit gaudia . . .

Welcome season
  with good reason:
spring restores our old delight:
  violets grow
  by the hedgerow,
sunshine renders all things bright:
so let care give way to fun —
  summer's coming,
  winter's running —
wicked winter's on the run!

Now withdrawing
  melting, thawing,
snow and ice and all the rest:
  mist has vanished,
  earth, long famished,
draws new life from spring's full breast:
dull and dreary, all who shun
  living, lusting,
  trysting, trusting
in the cheering summer sun!

Loudly voicing
  and rejoicing
we're all after Cupid's prize:
  we who win it
  find within it
sights reserved for lovers' eyes.
Venus orders — let's obey:
  loudly voicing
  and rejoicing,
we shall have her every day!

CB 145a   If . . .

Vvere div werlt alle min
von deme mere unze an den Rin . . .

If the whole wide world were mine
  from the sea up to the Rhine —
I would give it all a miss
  for a single night of bliss
    with the Queen of England!

CB 148   Flowers Unfurled

Floret tellus floribus
variis coloribus
  floret et cum gramine . . .

Flowers to their full unfurled
prettily bedeck the world
  greened again with grass anew:

may young men, to love subject,
hold in reverence and respect
  the requitals they pursue.

Grant that Venus may attend
all who call on her, and send
  Cupid to be present, too!

Youngsters earnest in their quest
may she suffer to be blessed
  with a lovers' rendezvous.

Venus – age-old, ever young –
sets her shafts to flight among
  her girls to love aspiring:

she who sees all lovers armed
never thwarted boys or harmed
  the girls of their desiring.

CB 149   Gone Away

Floret silva nobilis
floribus et foliis . . .

Forest, wood and lofty bower
flourishing with leaf and flower,
where is my once lover?
   Has he another?
He rode away to thwart me!
   Alas!
Now who will court me?

Floret silva undique
nah mime gesellen ist mir we!

CB 157   Sheep and Wolf: a Pastoral

Lucis orto sidere
exit virgo propere . . .

One day when dawn was on the wing
a girl as pretty as the spring
   sprang merrily from sleep,
and with her pastoral rod a-swing
   swung off to tend some sheep.

The sun attained its apogee
and beat down so unbearably
   this maid immaculate
was forced to find a shady tree,
   and there recuperate.

At this point I hove into view,
unlatched my tongue, and said 'Hulloo –
   is this a queen I see?
Behold, your slave! I beg of you,
   be generous to me!'

'Oh sir' (she cried) 'would you address
a damsel who, to her distress,
   has never known a man?
I've never met one, I confess,
   in all the fields I scan.'

By chance, there was a wolf around,
attracted to that happy sound –
   the bleats of woolly mutton:
it seized a sheep, and with a bound
   went off to play the glutton.

Distraught by evident distress,
'Alas!' declaimed my shepherdess
   in accents loud and shrill:
'Who saves my sheep fom vile duress
   may wive me at his will!'

'No sooner said than done,' I thought,
and with a sword that I had brought
   wroke vengeance on that cur –
so saved the sheep that had been caught
   and brought it back to her.

CB 158   Mid-Spring: a Pastoral

Vere dulci mediante,
non in Maio, paulo ante . . .

Mid-spring it was – well, not quite May:
a little bit before, I'd say –
when, lighted by the solar ray,
a girl, as lovely as the day
is long, stood where the green grass lay
    and trilled a reed-pipe sweetly.

Up came myself upon the scene.
A shapelier girl I'd never seen –
so well-distributed, I mean:
but as my sight was unforeseen
she shot away (plus sheep) to screen
    herself from me completely.

She screamed, and sought the pig-pen gate.
Hot in pursuit, I shouted 'Wait!
You needn't fear for your estate!'
I even offered her, as bait,
a necklace – which, sad to relate,
    she swore at indiscreetly.

'You stuff your baubles!' yelled the sprite:
'Lay off ! I know your sort, all right!' –
and grabbed her distaff for a fight.
I laid her low – and in that plight
she looked a more alluring sight
    for all her threadbare cover.

She didn't find the next bit fun –
though I thought it was nice, for one.
'You beast!' she cried: 'You should be hung

for what you've been and gone and done.
Still, since you have, just don't let on
   that you have been my lover.

'For if my dad found out — or my
big brother Martin — well, I'd lie
to say I wouldn't rather die.
And if it ever reached her, I
would find myself whipped soundly by
   the most horrendous mother!'

CB 167a Dance Song (1)

Swaz hie gat umbe
daz sint alles megede . . .

  Here, dancin' and a-whirlin',
  they're every one a virgin:
  they'll go without a man
  all summer if they can!

CB 174 Dance Song (2)

Veni, veni, venias,
ne me mori facias!

Come oh come oh come to me
or I die of misery!
Hyria, hyrie,
nazaza trillirivos!

Never saw a face so fair,
bright the eyes that sparkle there,
flowing waves of golden hair –
you're a picture past compare!

Redder than the rose's hue,
whiter than the lily's, too,
lovelier than all in view –
I will always worship you!

CB 174a   Dance Song (3)

Chume, chume, geselle min,
ih enbite harte din . . .

Come oh come my love to me,
    all too long I long for thee:
    all too long I long for thee:
come oh come my love to me.

With thy rose-red lips again
    come and cure me of my pain:
    come and cure me of my pain
with thy rose-red lips again.

CB 177   Girl in a Red Dress

Stetit puella
rufa tunica . . .

There was a girl who had
a tunic of bright red:
if anyone touched her
they'd set that dress astir!
        Aha!

She stood upon her toes
just like a little rose:
her face shone bright and fair:
and red lips blossomed there –
     Aha!

The girl just stood there – she
was right beside a tree –
and amorously wrote
her love a little note.
     Aha!

Then Venus chanced to pass
and wished her '*Caritas!* –
may the one you cleave to
love you and never leave you' –
     Aha!

CB 178   Love in Return

Volo virum vivere   viriliter;
diligam si diligar   equaliter . . .

I maintain a man was made
    for manliness:
so I'll love, but only if
    loved none the less;
that's the only kind of love
    I count correct –
and I'll outdo Jupiter
    in this respect:
I won't seek to buy her,
    use vulgar coin to try her:
maybe I'll become her man –
    but first, I'll be loved by her.

There's a pride from which no woman
    is exempt,
and I'll give as it deserves –
    profound contempt.
Why should I wait for my suit
    to take its course?
Am I one to ride my cart
    before her horse?
  Fools indulge this craving –
  my views on them are scathing!
cast me as her player, but
    not as her cast-off plaything.

If she cares to please me – well,
    I will respond:
let her first be fond of me,
    I will be fond:
that's the only game I'll play –
    no loss, no gain –
lest she count me as the chaff,
    herself the grain.
  I accept love's traces –
  but on an equal basis:
I have little patience with
    a lady's airs and graces.

Freedom is my middle name –
    I boast it thus!
and I live more chastely than
    Hippolytus.
Let no woman think she'll just
    seduce me by
wagging her pretty finger or
    winking an eye:
  she must love sincerely
  and say I please her really:
that's the kind of forwardness
    that suits a woman dearly!

Oh my love, my love – this song
    displeases me,
and I find its sentiment
    un-eases me.
Lady, see me subject to
    thy loveliness,
who ignored thine elegance
    and now confess.
  Pardoned – no I can't be
for acting ungallantly:
punish, pray, thy penitent –
  but in thy bedroom, grant me.

CB 179   Playtime

Tempus est iocundum
   o virgines!
modo congaudete
   vos iuvenes!

Out you come – it's playtime,
  you girls again!
Join them in the May-time,
  young gentlemen!

Oh, oh!
merrily we go!
now I have a lover who
has set my heart aglow:
novel, novel is the love
that slays me, oh!

Nightingales are singing
  delightfully:
melodiously trilling
  their hearts away!

Oh, oh! . . .

She that I adore so —
   none lovelier!
like a rose but more so —
   I'd die for her!

Oh, oh! . . .

Promises you make me
   are ecstasy!
But when you forsake me
   they're agony!

Oh, oh! . . .

How can I have fun if
   I'm innocent?
How I am undone if
   I'm ignorant!

Oh, oh! . . .

Nightingale, cease singing
   a moment long —
for my heart is bringing
   itself to song.

Oh, oh! . . .

In the winter season
   we're serious —
when the sap has risen
   lascivious!

Oh, oh! . . .

Come, with joy complying:
   renew my love!
come along – I'm dying
   for you, my love!

Oh, oh! . . .

CB 180   Apple of my Eye

O mi dilectissima,
vultu serenissima . . .

O you apple of my eye –
you and your sweet smile! – now try
this little test, and tell me true
who these lines are written to!
  Lack-a-day, lack-a-day,
  will she never come my way?

'Who is she, delightful girl?'
(I asked myself) 'This lustrous pearl
in whose features fair and bright
the red rose tussles with the white?'
  Lack-a-day . . .

Written in your lovely face
is all of breeding, all of grace:
milk of kindness in your breast
vies with passions unsuppressed.
  Lack-a-day . . .

Who is this young lady, who,
sweeter than the honeydew?
So intense I feel about her
I can hardly live without her.
    Lack-a-day . . .

Down inside the soul of me
sighs consume the whole of me —
oh, for all your loveliness,
source of all my heart's distress.
    Lack-a-day . . .

How the sparkling of your eyes
dims the sun that scours the skies —
as the lightning streak that flings
brightness down on shadowed things.
    Lack-a-day . . .

May the gods of love be kind
to this plan I have in mind:
shatter to nihility
her chains of virginity.
    Lack-a-day . . .

CB 183   Curing Timidity

Si puer cum puellula
moraretur in cellula —
    felix conjunctio!

If ever boy and girl presume
to linger in a little room —
    Happy communion!
    As yearning grows to burning
    they'll find a remedy
    to cure them of timidity!

Into a thrilling game they fall
of lips and legs and limbs and all . . .
    Happy communion!
    As yearning grows to burning
    they'll find a remedy
    to cure them of timidity!

CB 185   Under the Linden Tree

Ich was ein chint so wolgetan
  virgo dum florebam . . .

Oh, what a lovely girl I was
    when I was young and pure!
Everyone thought the world of me –
    I charmed them, to be sure!

    Alas and lack-a-day!
  Thrice cursèd be the linden tree
    that grows along the way!

One day I went off to the fields
    to pluck me a bouquet:
but a vagabond lay there, with plans
    to pluck ME, so to say!

    Alas . . .

He took me by the fair white hand –
    not without hesitation –
and led me to the field himself –
    with some prevarication.

    Alas . . .

He then grabbed at my nice white dress
   very indecently,
and gripped me harder by the hand –
   excruciatingly.

Alas . . .

He murmured 'Come along, my girl:
   these woods look good enough.'
'But as for me, I hate this route!'
   I cried, and all that stuff.

Alas . . .

'Under a tallish linden tree,
   not very far from hence,
you'll find I've left a lovely lute –
   and suchlike instruments.'

Alas . . .

But when we reached that linden tree
   he said 'Here's where we'll sit –'
(He was a-quiver with desire!) –
   'Let's play around a bit.'

Alas . . .

With that, he seized me bodily –
   not without nervousness –
and said 'I'd like to marry you –
   you've got a pretty face!'

Alas . . .

Then tearing off my little gown
   he bared me pink as ham
and battered down my last defence
   with a rampant battering-ram!

Alas . . .

Up with his bow and arrows then –
   how well his hunt did go!
For he had played me false, and won.
   'Thanks, darling. Cheerio!'

Alas . . .

CB 186   Avowal

Suscipe, Flos, florem
quia flos designat amorem . . .

I
Take thou this flower, O Flower,
as love's most faithful avower:
which selfsame flower
enfolds me in its power:
for always, Flora, inspire
its odour, dearest desire:
who come with brightness adorning
to rival the splendour of morning.
Gaze on this flower, O Flora,
and smile upon thine adorer:
incline to its delicate treasure:
thy voice is the nightingale's pleasure.
And kiss this perfection of posies:
red lips blend well with roses.

II
    Roses in depiction
are faithless as a fiction:
    who paints the bloom
forswears its true perfume.

III
Drinking and Gaming Songs

CB 191   The Archpoet's Confession

Estuans intrinsecus   ira vehementi
in amaritudine   loquor meë menti . . .

1
Boiling over in the mind,
   angry indignation
bitterly impels me to
   self-examination:
made of earthly elements,
   dusty and decaying,
I am like a leaf the wind
   tosses in its playing.

2
Since the unmistakable
   mark of one of wisdom
is to build upon a rock
   following a system
I must be a simpleton —
   like a winding river,
never holding to a course,
   deviating ever.

3
Like a boat without a crew
   I'm forever drifting —

or a bird upon the blue
   when the wind is lifting.
Chains have never shackled me
   neither keys confined me:
I consort with rabble who
   take me as they find me.

4

I believe a serious mien
   means a serious weakness:
having fun's a finer thing,
   more than honey-sweetness.
Venus keeps me occupied
   in a job I much like –
one she never offers to
   sobersides and suchlike.

5

Broad's the path I slither down,
   young at heart's the fashion:
virtue leaves me cold – but vice
   stimulates my passion.
self-indulgence I desire,
   rather than salvation:
dead my soul, my flesh deserves
   sole consideration.

6

Give, O reverend my Lord,
   ear to my confession:
it's a goodly death I die,
   sweet is my secession –
dying, as I am, for girls
   oozing with temptation:
those I can't possess, I'll take
   in imagination.

7

Can the leopard change his spots?
   so it strains at nature
not to lust when smitten by
   some enchanting creature.
Being young, we can't comply
   with austere conjurements –
for there's no known antidote
   to feminine allurements.

8

Who, committed to the flames,
   goes without a burning?
Who, ensconced in Pavia,
   seeks a chaste sojourning? –
where Venus with come-hither eyes
   and cheeks adorned for rapture
crooks a finger to secure
   another youthful capture?

9

Put Hippolytus himself
   in a like location
and a day or two will see
   such a transformation!
Here, all roads lead not to Rome
   but to my lady's chamber:
bedrooms, bedrooms, everywhere –
   but not a place to slumber.

10

Secondly, I stand accused
   of dicey entertainment.
Well, supppose a cast or two
   did rob me of my raiment?

Outside, I could feel the cold –
   inside, I was sweating
at the anvil of my art:
   better verse begetting.

11
Item Three against me reads
   'TAVERN'. I won't skirt it.
Since I never passed one by,
   now I shan't desert it –
not, at least, till I'm assured
   the heavenly choir has started
droning '*Requiem aeternam*'
   for this dear departed.

*

12
In a tavern I intend,
   when time is called, to snuff it –
near enough to lots of wine
   for dying lips to quaff it:
then may the angelic host
   chant in all its glory
'*Sit Deus propitius
   huic potatori . . .*'

13
May the lantern of my soul,
   flushed with tankard's fire,
pickled in sweet alcohol,
   to the stars retire:
nothing beats a tavern wine –
   it renders me more zealous
than the stuff they water down
   in your Lordship's cellars.

14

Poets who profess to spurn
    populated places
lock themselves in hidey-holes
    from prying eyes and faces:
study and apply themselves,
    labour till they shrivel —
all to yield a waiting world
    a masterpiece of drivel.

15

Let them fast! Let them abstain!
    Let choruses of poets
waft above the daily brawl
    and live like little stoics.
Let them linger in their cells
    labouring and fasting —
dying to promote their names
    to glory everlasting!

16

Every one of us is born
    with his own endowment:
writing in a state of fast
    isn't *my* avowment:
hungry, I'm an easy match
    for any schoolboy jelly —
I would rather fill a grave
    than feel an empty belly.

17

Every one of us is born
    with his own advantage:
I, engaged in writing verse,
    sup a goodly vintage:

nothing but the very best
  on the wine-list showing
kindles my creativeness,
  gets me really going.

18

The more I drink, the more I write –
  that's the plain equation:
I'm incapable of work,
  suffering starvation:
empty stomach, empty words,
  worthless rightly reckoned –
ah! but when I've had a bit
  Ovid comes off second!

19

Never did the flighty muse
  titivate my pages
till my stomach had received
  something of its wages:
not before Lord Bacchus reigns
  over my endeavour
can Apollo sparkle me
  into something clever.

*

20

See me, sinner self-confessed,
  I myself admitting
all the wrongs your Peeping Toms
  accuse me of committing.
Note that none of them are damned
  by their own exertions –
though they share a weakness for
  secular diversions.

21

See me of my own accord
    in your worthy presence
beg you do the Bible's will
    nor deny its essence:
anyone who finds his heart
    free of sin can show it –
let him be the first to cast
    a stone upon your poet.

22

I confess to everything,
    everything against me:
spit the poison out, which long
    cankered and incensed me:
shame attends my former life,
    hope the paths that guide me:
men see me, but only God
    can see the heart inside me.

23

I will cleave to righteousness,
    sinful ways abhorring:
feel the spirit rise again
    to my soul's restoring:
be a little babe in arms
    innocently feeding –
lest I'm led astray again
    by the world's misleading.

24

Dignitary of Cologne,
    here is my petition:
that your mercy shine on me
    is my sole ambition:

favour with a penance me
  whom you hear confessing:
let me do as you desire,
  and count it as a blessing.

25

When the lion, king of beasts,
  sees his subjects cowering,
even he inclines to spare
  and moderates his glowering;
pray you, Princes, do the same –
  for all your earthly glitter,
one who's never sweet remains
  devilishly bitter.

CB 193   Wine and Water in Debate

Denudata veritate
succinctaque brevitate
  ratione varia . . .

1

Hear the truth! It's plain, unvarnished,
by long-windedness untarnished,
  and improved by various quotes:
Never mix in the same pitcher
substances together which are
  always at each other's throats.

2

There are those who like to mingle
wine and water in a single
  jug – but such togetherness
isn't to be advocated:
one should rather have it rated
  an unmitigated mess.

3

For the wine goes not to water
as a lamb might to the slaughter
    but demands indignantly:
'Scram! Get lost! Go to perdition!
Who on earth gave you permission
    to enjoy my company?

4

'Water – only fit for throwing
down the drain, forever flowing
    in a filthy sort of flood:
all you want, you vile and vicious
substance, is to crawl down fissures
    and degenerate to mud.

5

'What do you add to a table?
Neither host nor guest feels able
    to converse with you around:
even he once hale and hearty,
life and soul of every party,
    hardly dares to make a sound.

6

'All who drink of you too freely,
though quite healthy, soon grow mealy
    thanks to your disruptive strains:
bellies churn: wind in compression,
bottled up, denied expression,
    fills them with appalling pains.

7

'When the belly's full of wind, it
does its utmost to rescind it
    fore and aft, as well it should:

though thereby it may bestill wind,
none the less it makes an ill wind
    that blows no one any good.'

8

Water now, with anger straining,
counters: '*You* require explaining,
    fount of evil, source of cares:
they who quaff wine lean to quarrels,
waste their lives and let their morals
    slither downhill unawares.

9

'They're incapable of talking –
totter home instead of walking –
    all who labour at your lips:
words they hear without discerning –
see a hundred lanterns burning
    at the sight of two small dips.

10

'Who then are your advocators?
Murderers and fornicators!
    Tom, Dick, Harry and the dregs!
Guttersnipes expound your praises
in the most sententious phrases
    to a court of vats and kegs!

11

'No one treats you like a freeman:
rightly counting you a demon,
    vintners lock you up in vats.
I, however, take my pleasure
strolling through the world at leisure,
    free of cares and caveats.

12

'I save folk from desiccation,
while to souls who seek salvation
    my necessity is clear:
for I offer pilgrims leeway
far and wide to ply my freeway
    to the shrines they most revere.'

13

Wine retorts: 'You can't believe in
what you say: it's self-deceiving.
    True, I grant, you may sustain
a ship or two. But then you riot,
batter them, and won't lie quiet
    till they're wrecked in your domain.

14

'Anybody who can't drink you
so completely as to shrink you
    rides in peril on the sea –
so they sink, who trusted on you:
who dares pilgrimage upon you
    journeys to eternity.

15

'I'm a god. I call as witness
Ovid, no less, to my fitness
    at inspiring one and all
to wisdom. Lecturers, abstaining,
lose their faculty of explaining –
    students spurn that lecture hall!

16

'Only one who founds his thinking
on (unwatered) wine for drinking
    can distinguish false from true.

Deaf to hearing, dumb to talking,
blind to seeing, lame to walking,
   sad to laughing, I renew.

17

'Wine sees life through old men surging –
water leaves youth with its urging
   withered and by age defiled.
I keep populations thriving –
with you, no amount of writhing
   gets a woman with a child.'

18

'God?' (says Water) 'Yes – one who can
lead a saint astray, as few can,
   down the path from bad to worse:
you can teach how to dissemble
till the wisest judge resemble
   Doubting Thomas Didymus.

19

'God? Oh yes, God of damnation,
double-dealing, dissipation,
   ills and evils sprung from you:
you destroy good men completely,
then you slink away discreetly
   when pure water springs to view.

20

'Here's a truth you'll find instructive:
only I can make productive
   woods and gardens, fields and bowers:
for when drought comes, greens and grasses
die away, the fresh bloom passes
   from the face of leaves and flowers.

21

'Poor old mother Vine, distorted,
finds her would-be grapes aborted,
    falls to barren disarray:
crawls along the desiccated
ground, bald and defoliated,
    wanly there to waste away.

22

'In my absence, dire starvation
overwhelms a population
    weeping inconsolably:
Christians, Jews and unbelievers
on their knees like eager beavers
    pray the swift return of me.'

23

Wine retorts: 'Your fulsome praises
come across as empty phrases –
    other viewpoints might be got:
everybody knows you favour
stinking sewers' filthy flavour –
    don't you think we know what's what?

24

'All the waste of all who live is
thrown at you from bogs and privies:
    you bear off – what's best inferred.
Filth and faeces, lurid liquid –
you knock back what I'd be sick with . . .
    I'm lost for another word!'

25

Water, welling up with anger,
interrupts the wicked slander
    and expostulates to Wine:

'Glory be for revelation
of this god's denomination –
  hear its utterance divine!

26

'I'm immune to your derision –
though such rudeness spoils the vision
  of all that a god might say.
I, before I've gone ten paces,
dissipate the final traces
  of the filth I've borne away.'

27

Wine replies: 'Your finely spoken
argument's a worthless token
  for the facts give you away:
many fall to grave disorder
from contaminated water,
  dying off within the day!'

28

Overcome by Wine's offences,
Water took leave of her senses –
  numbed and dumbstruck, wept and sighed.
'What?' says Wine. 'No more excuses?
Wine's the winner: Water loses:
  one can see you're stupefied!'

29

I (your poet, Peter) now de-
clare a finish to this rowdy
  dispute. Here's the final score:
Whoso join these two together
may Christ from salvation sever
  always and for evermore.

AMEN

CB 196 In the Tavern

In taberna quando sumus
non curamus, quid sit humus . . .

In the tavern when we're drinking,
though the ground be cold and stinking,
down we get to join the action
with the dice-controlling faction:
what goes on inside the salon –
where it's strictly cash per gallon –
if you'd like to know, sir, well you
shut your mouth and I shall tell you.

Some are boozing, some are playing,
some a coarser side displaying:
most of those who like to gamble
wind up naked in the scramble:
some emerge attired in new things,
some in bits and bobs and shoestrings:
no one thinks he'll kick the bucket
dicing for a beery ducat.

First to them with cash to wallow in,
then we layabouts toast the following:
second, drink to all held captive,
thirdly drink to those still active,
fourthly drink to the Christian-hearted,
fifthly drink to the dear departed,
sixthly to our free-and-easy sisters,
seventhly to all unemployed enlisters.

Eighthly drink to friars deconverted,
ninthly, monks from monast'ries diverted,
tenthly, sailors of the oceans,
eleventhly, louts who cause commotions,

twelfthly, those who wear the penitential,
thirteenth, and whose journey is essential —
to this fat pope, to that thin king —
who the hell cares why they're drinking!

Drinking tinker, drinking tailor,
drinking soldier, drinking sailor,
drinking rich man, drinking poor man,
drinking beggarman, thief and lawman:
drinking servant, drinking master,
drinking mistress, drinking pastor,
drinking doctor, drinking layman,
drinking drunkard, drinking drayman,

Drinking rude man, drinking proper,
drinking tiddler, drinking whopper,
drinking scholar, drinking gypsy,
drinking drunk or maudlin tipsy:
drinking father, drinking mother,
drinking sister, drinking brother,
drinking husbands, wives and lovers,
and a hundred thousand others —

Half a million pounds would never
purchase what we drink together,
for we drink beyond all measure,
purely for the sake of pleasure:
so you see us, poor and shoddy,
criticized by everybody —
God grant that they be confounded
when at last the trump is sounded!

CB 197 The Tavern's Lantern

Dum domus lapidea
foro sita cernitur . . .

When the tavern's crystalline
lantern lights the market place,
shimmering with nasal shine
from many a brother's rosy face –
'Here we are!' cries everyone:
'This looks like a bag of fun.'
   Bacchus drily –
   Venus slyly –
snatches students in a snare:
   for a bob or
   two they'll rob or
hock the very coats they wear.

As we're taught by appetite,
   let's begin to
   get stuck into
food for – not thought, but – delight.
   Then to wine we'll expedite.

O how welcome wine is! – Wine, the antidote
to all our watery storms of hurt and doubt,
   instils between the lips of those half cut
such ecstasy as ever love poured out.

   Bacchus kindly minds us:
   unflagging flagons finds us
of gentle wine mellifluous in flavour,
outstanding for its nectar-sodden savour:
and endless rounds and rounds of it go turning
to blot our troubles out of all discerning . . .

... 'Come on then,' cries everyone, 'let's scarper
now our appetites are that much sharper:
bellies balk at foodless drink – it puts them in a flummock:
a booze-up's only half the fun upon an empty stomach.'

They stagger from the inn with cheers and waving
and tumble forth upon the weed-grown paving:
brother drinkers, bare-backed in the clover,
devoutly genuflect, and topple over.
Down in the mud they murmur 'Let us pray!'
But then – 'Arise!' they hear somebody, *a posteriori*, say:
'You've earned a favourable response to your petition –
for Bacchus can't fail to be touched by your contrite position!'

CB 207   Verses on Dice

Tessera, blandita fueras michi . . .
Tessera materies est . . .
Sunt comites ludi . . .
Hi tres ecce canes . . .

I
Dice, you were kind to me once
when I still had cash to my name:
Dice, now I've been double-crossed –
I'm lost! You're entirely to blame!

II
Dice are the root and branch of
every deterioration:
Dice degrade humankind, con-
found divine aspiration.

III
Guess who accompany gaming? –
Trickery, Trumpery, Shaming,
Breaking-of-pledges, and Theft,
and Having-no-property-left.

IV
These are my hounds, my three dice:
Swift, Slothful, Hardly-Precise:
    in them I trust
    to earn me a crust
and double or triple my price.

Property, mortgages, fee,
estates with fine houses – these three
    sniff out with a view
    to extracting from you
thus rendering service to me!

CB210   Verses on Chess

Qui cupit egregium   scachorum noscere ludum,
  Audiat: ut potui   carmine composui . . .

All who desire instruction
in chess, most noble distraction,
    hark: I've written you these
    ditties of expertise.

First, a few lines to settle
the scene of this sportive battle.
    The board measures eight by eight
    and bi-coloured squares alternate.

White is the usual colour
of one, and red is the other —
   failing red, black or blue
   or any old colour will do.

Rooks in the first position
threaten their warlike commission:
   on each next square, a knight
   champs at the bit for a fight.

On the third square stands a bishop
on guard against royal mishap:
   king on the fourth is seen
   standing next to his queen.

Then follow, up to the border,
the same men but in reverse order —
   and on the subsequent row
   little pawns, raring to go.

They proceed down the wide ways
capturing, right or left, sideways,
   adverse pieces that stand
   on each diagonal hand.

Should any pawn's expedition
reach to the eighthmost position
   it drops the pawn's routine,
   takes on that of a queen.

Having thus changed its sex, it
fights for its monarch — protects it,
   orders and regulates:
   here conquers, and there abates.

Pawns, as the first to engage in
battle, fall first to its raging,
  leaving a pathway clear
  for those in wait at the rear.

Rooks, let loose by their slaughter,
roam over every quarter,
  marching wherever they may
  if nothing stands in their way.

Major pieces take major,
threaten the minor with danger –
  yet even they may fall
  prey to the weakest of all.

Bearing the signs of his knighting,
swift, wise, and clever at fighting,
  see the bold knight advance
  seizing his every chance.

Capturing innocent pieces
who lack his subtle caprices:
  worrying this way and that,
  here lays low – there is laid flat.

As for the bishop, his three-pointed
headgear leaves courage disjointed:
  hither and thither he goes
  felling invigilant foes.

Dominant pieces put paid to
minor pieces – yet they, too,
  yield to the weakest of all.
  Pawns are the quickest to fall.

No king can ever be taken
although by his partner forsaken:
  queenless, her king and lord
  has to remain on the board.

Often a king, though surrounded
by aides, is 'checkmated' or grounded:
  if he has nowhere to flee
  that is the finish of he.

CB216   Rag Day

Tempus hoc letitie
dies festus hodie! . . .

Hooray! Today's a holiday:
a happy day – a jolly day:
a day to strum guitars and play
the good old songs the good old way:
to love your neighbour and display
the side of you that's bright and gay:
and students most of all, for they
excel at parties anyway!

So throw your books and slates away –
there's food for which you needn't pay:
forget the works of Ovid, eh? –
and tell his friends to go and play.
Never mind what people say
  youth needs its recreations:
since the world is making hay
  let's join the celebrations!

CB219   The Venerable Order of Vagrants

Cum 'In orbem universum'   decantatur 'ite',
sacerdotes ambulant,   currunt cenobite . . .

1

'Go ye into all the world . . .'
  hear the text – it's stunning!
Simple clerics saunter up,
  novices come running,
deacons from their lecterns rise,
  relinquishing their reading,
avid for the healthy life
  our sect is known for leading.

2

'Try all things . . .': the text inspires
  our Order's regulations:
if you'd like to try our way,
  first try these exhortations:
crafty clergy and false priests
  turn your other side on –
they're the ones whose charity
  can never be relied on.

3

Be you Margrave, Austrian,
  Bavarian or Saxon –
I implore you, friend, however
  noble your extraction,
listen to the new decretals
  recently propounded:
'Perish penny-pinchers all
  and skinflints be confounded!'

4

Look at us: we surely are
   the fount of all compassion,
welcoming both high and low
   and in and out of fashion,
taking both the richest and
   most destitute of mortals —
even those the godly monks
   leave starving at their portals.

5

Gladly we admit the monk
   with tonsure neatly shaven:
presbyters — their wives as well —
   will find in us a haven:
plus the teacher and his class,
   the servant and his master —
as for scholars, if well-dressed
   perhaps a little faster.

6

Welcome to our Order are
   the righteous and the wrong 'uns,
the blind, the halt, the hunched of back,
   the healthy and the strong 'uns:
youngsters in the bloom of youth
   and oldsters who eschew it:
those who balk at venery
   and such as overdo it.

7

Bellicose or pacifist,
   meek or mad as hatter:
Roman, Slav, Bohemian —
   or German — doesn't matter:

men of mediocre height
   as well as dwarfs and giants –
whether self-effacing types
   or bristling with defiance.

8

Note that we're an *Order* when
   applying for admission:
you'll not be refused on grounds
   of race, rank or position:
though you *hic* or *hike* or *hock*
   when out upon a bender
you can only be declined
   by number and by gender.

9

Now for the monastic rules
   of Venerable Vagrants –
yes, a venerable life,
   and sweet as any fragrance!
One in which a juicy steak
   is rather to our pleasure
than the mouldy grain that monks
   provide in measly measure.

10

In our Order, matins are
   explicitly forbidden:
that's when phantoms roam abroad –
   it's wiser to stay hidden;
phantoms tend to scare the pants
   off one, although they're sham – and
if you rise at crack of dawn
   you'll need your head examined.

11

Matins having been denied
   by the Order's motions,
we on rising seek the nearest
   inn for our devotions:
there with wine to quench our thirst –
   and fowl to quench our hunger –
nothing scares one half so much
   as casting a wrong number.

12

By our rules, the right to wear
   two layers is abolished:
if you own a tunic, you're
   presentable and polished –
throw away your surplus surplice,
   then get down to dicing,
with your belt as next in line
   to the sacrificing.

13

Now, below the belt you'll find
   a further motto, which is:
if you have a shirt to lose
   why bother about breeches?
As for boots – if boots there be,
   your shoes can be donated.
Disobey these rules, and you'll
   be excommunicated!

14

Never leave the table with
   a tum in need of filling.
Short of cash? Then borrow some
   from anyone who's willing:

often, when Dame Fortune takes
   a fancy to a punter,
one coin wins enough to over-
   whelm a fortune-hunter!

15

Never bend against the wind
   in your peregrinations,
nor let a sad countenance
   proclaim your deprivations:
let your faith be fortified
   with confidence a-plenty
and 'Your sorrow shall be turned
   to joy!' (John, 16, 20).

16

Everyone you come across
   must understand your mission:
say your function is to test
   their moral disposition:
say 'I'm sent to segregate
   the pure from the improper –
to reprimand the reprobate
   and approbate the proper.'

CB 222   The Abbot of Cockaigne

Ego sum abbas Cucaniensis . . .

I am the abbot of Cockaigne,
and I take counsel with my drinking companions,
and my persuasion is that of the gambling fraternity,
and if anyone consults me in the tavern at matins,
come vespers, he'll have lost the shirt off his back:
and being thus fleecèd of his raiment will cry –

'Save me! Save me!
What have you done, god-forsaken dice?
Now you've made me sacrifice
all I knew of paradise!'

Supplement

CB 2* My Lady Love

Ich lob die liben frowen min
vor allen gvten wiben . . .

I will extol my lady love
  above the best of others
and in her service I shall prove
  the faithfullest of lovers:
  she like a looking-glass
or diamond of the finest class
engages with such excellence
  I lose all sense of sense.

Her rose-red lips evoke in me
  the longings of a lover:
her eyes sparkle incessantly
  like stars through cloudy cover:
  her hand alone constrains
my heart – she has no need of chains.
I never saw such loveliness –
  an angel in the flesh.

My life is hers, to loose, to hold –
  such is the vow I make her.
With her I'll happily grow old
  and never yet forsake her.
  She will? Then well and good:
I'll live to serve her as I should.
If not, let me take leave of life
  and endless woe to wife.

CB 16*   Mary Magdalene's Song
(From a Passion Play)

Chramer, gip die varwe mier,
  div min wengel roete . . .

> Chapman, let me have some rouge
>   made for my complexion:
> so that I may lead young men
>   willy-nilly
>   into my affection.
>
>   *Look at me,*
>   *young man — see:*
>   *let me be your pleasure!*
>
> Sir, you are required to love
>   ladies who deserve it:
> true love elevates the heart:
>   people honour
>   gentlemen who serve it.
>
>   *Look at me,*
>   *young man — see:*
>   *let me be your pleasure!*
>
> Bless you, World, for your joys:
>   how shall I repay you?
> Let me plight my troth to you —
>   in your service
>   honour and obey you.
>
>   *Look at me,*
>   *young man — see:*
>   *let me be your pleasure!*

CB3*   Winter Time

Iam dudum estivalia
pertransiere tempora . . .

It hardly seems the other day
that summer rose and went its way.
    Bitter winter, iron-grey,
downcasts us by its drab display.
    Rain and snow and hailstones prey
upon the mind and lead astray
to desolation and dismay.

Poor little birds sit silently
who practised once from tree to tree
    each his proper melody,
revelling in minstrelsy.
    Earth lies stripped of greenery:
the sun reflects half-heartedly
on days that briefly dawn, then flee.

One lacks the strength to satisfy
what Venus should be worshipped by:
    such enthusiasms die
when warmth has waned and chill is nigh.
    May they curse you and defy
you, Winter, who with Spring did lie
and found her trades a joy to ply.

From woods and glades where lovers go
for conversation sweet and low
    vows to females apropos
have vanished with the winds that blow.
    To the season we forgo
be all the gratitude we owe
and glory *in perpetuo*.

Since gentle summertime withdrew
for winter's tempests to ensue,
    melancholicly we view
the sorry state we've fallen to.
    Springtime, may you soon renew
with swift return those faithful who
so long lament the loss of you.

APPENDICES

APPENDICES

Appendix A
Concert Arrangement

This is an English-language version of the selection used in Orff's cantata. Inevitable discrepancies occur between these and the foregoing translations. They arise partly because Orff worked from an earlier edition of the text, making further abridgements and alterations of his own, and partly because the English is intended to be singable, which calls for additional compromise between sound and sense.

O Fortuna
CB 17 (complete)

O how Fortune,
inopportune,
apes the moon's inconstancy:
waxing, waning,
losing, gaining,
life treats us detestably:
first oppressing
then caressing
shifts us like pawns in her play:
destitution,
restitution,
mixes and melts them away.

Fate, as vicious
as capricious,
whirling your merry-go-round:
evil doings,
worthless wooings,

crumble away to the ground:
   darkly stealing,
   unrevealing,
working against me you go:
   for your measure
   of foul pleasure
I bare my back to your blow.

   Noble actions,
   true transactions,
no longer fall to my lot:
   powers to make me
   then to break me
all play their part in your plot:
   now seize your time –
   waste no more time,
pluck these poor strings and let go:
   since the strongest
   fall the longest
let the world share in my woe.

Fortune plango vulnera
CB 16   (complete)

I cry the cruel cuts of Fate
   with eyes worn red from weeping,
whose fickle favours travel straight
   back into her keeping:
as ye read, so shall ye find –
   luck comes curly-headed
from the front, but round behind
   not a hair is threaded!

Dame Fortune once invited me
   to enjoy her blessing:
to riches' throne exalted me,
   caring and caressing:

but from maximum renown,
   garlanded and fêted,
Fate stepped up and threw me down –
   glory dissipated!

Fortune's wheel goes round and round,
   down go all my talents;
others rising from the ground
   fly too high to balance:
so beware Fate's old routine,
   kings and lords and ladies –
for beneath her throne lies Queen
   Hecuba in Hades.

Veris leta facies
CB 138   (stanzas 1, 2, 4)

Spring unveils herself again,
   smiling on creation:
Winter's rule of wind and rain
   falls in ruination:
gaily garlanded and crowned,
   Flora bids adherence:
birds rejoice and woods resound
   at her reappearance.

Phoebus with his sunny smile
   cleaves to Flora's breast –
both anew in flowery style
   colourfully dressed:
Zephyrus eke with sweet breath
   warmly wafts above us,
while we strive, as to the death,
   for the prize of lovers.

Charmingly the nightingale
   whiles away the hours:
meadows merrily regale
   all the world with flowers:
from the woods the bird-flock whirls
   myriads of flights —
while a dancing ring of girls
   hints of greater heights.

Omnia sol temperat

CB 136   (complete)

Sunshine overrules the world
   peaceably and purely:
April with her veil unfurled
   bares herself demurely;
now to thoughts of love anew
   everyone confesses,
gladsomely surrend'ring to
   Eros's caresses.

Spring inspiring once a year
   Nature's new condition
bids us follow with good cheer
   in the old tradition:
may the springtime of your youth
   lead you to discover
need to rest in trust and truth
   faithful to your lover.

Therefore love me faithfully,
   mark my own devotion:
may it be whole-heartedly
   and with resolution.
I am with you everywhere
   far away though wending:
all who love as I, must bear
   agonies unending.

Ecce, gratum
CB 143 (complete)

Welcome, season,
with good reason:
spring restores our old delight:
violets grow
by the hedgerow,
sunshine renders all things bright:
so may care give way to fun –
summer's coming,
winter's running –
nasty winter's on the run!

Now withdrawing,
melting, thawing,
snow and ice and all the rest:
mists are vanished,
earth, half famished,
draws new life from summer's breast:
dull and dreary all who shun
living, lusting,
trysting, trusting
in the cheery summer sun!

Loudly voicing
and rejoicing
we're all after Cupid's prize:
we who win it
see within it
sights reserved for lovers' eyes;
Venus orders – let's obey:
loudly voicing
and rejoicing,
we shall have her every day!

Floret silva nobilis

CB 149   (complete; and repeated in German)

> Forest, wood and lofty bower,
> flourishing with leaf and flower,
> where is my once lover?
>   has he another?
> He went away and left me . . .
>   Alas!
> Now who will love me?

Chramer, gip die varwe mier

Three of the verses sung by Mary Magdalene
in the passion play numbered CB 16*

> Chapman, let me have some rouge
>   made for my complexion:
> so that I may lead young men
>   willy-nilly
>   into my affection.
>
>   *Look at me,*
>   *young man – see:*
>   *let me be your pleasure!*
>
> Sir, you are required to love
>   ladies who deserve it:
> true love elevates the heart:
>   people honour
>   gentlemen who serve it.
>
> Bless you, World, for your joys:
>   how shall I repay you?
> Let me plight my troth to you,
>   in your service
>   honour and obey you.

Swaz hie gat umbe
CB 167a   (complete)

Here, dancin' and a-whirlin',
they're every one a virgin:
they plan to go without a man
all the summer if they can!

Chume, chume, geselle min
CB 174a   (complete; the German-language appendix to
'*Veni, veni, venias*')

Come oh come my love to me
all too long I long for thee:
all too long I long for thee
come oh come my love to me.

With thy rose-red lips again
come and cure me of my pain:
come and cure me of my pain
with thy rose-red lips again.

Were diu werlt alle min
CB 145a   (complete)

If the whole wide world were mine
from the sea as far as the Rhine
I'd exchange its countless charms
I'd exchange its countless charms
for one chance of lying in the arms,
of lying in the arms
of Eleanor of England!

Estuans interius
CB 191   (stanzas 1–5)

Boiling over in the mind
    anger and aggression
bitterly impel me to
    make you my confession:
made of earthly elements,
    dusty and decaying,
I am like a leaf the wind
    tosses in its playing.

Since the unmistakable
    mark of one of wisdom
is to build upon a rock
    following a system
see in me a simpleton,
    like a winding river,
never holding to a course,
    deviating ever.

Like a boat without a crew
    I'm for ever drifting,
or a bird upon the blue
    when the wind is lifting;
chains have never shackled me,
    never key confined me:
I consort with rabble who
    take me as they find me.

Seems to me, a serious mien
    means a serious weakness:
fun's a finer thing by far,
    more than honey-sweetness:
Venus keeps me occupied
    in a task I much like –
one she never offers to
    sobersides and suchlike.

Wide's the road I travel down,
   young at heart's the fashion:
virtue leaves me cold – but then
   vice excites my passion:
self-indulgence I desire
   rather than salvation:
dead my soul, my flesh deserves
   sole consideration.

Olim lacus colueram
CB 130   (stanzas 1, 3, 5)

Once I had lakes to live upon:
in glory I would swim along –
once, when I used to be a swan.

  Poor thing, poor thing –
    not a raw thing
    but done like anything!

Cook on the spit is curving me,
flames sear through every nerve in me –
now here's a waiter serving me!

Here in this serving dish I lie
where I have no power to fly –
and grinding molars greet the eye.

Ego sum abbas
CB 222   (complete)

I am the abbot of Cockaigne,
and I take counsel with my drinking companions,
and my persuasion is that of the gambling fraternity,
and if anyone consults me in the tavern at matins,
come vespers, he'll have lost the shirt off his back:

and being thus fleecèd of his raiment will cry –
'Save me! Save me!
What have you done, god-forsaken dice?
Now you've made me sacrifice
all I knew of paradise!'

In taberna quando sumus
CB 196   (complete)

In the tavern when we're drinking,
though the ground be cold and stinking,
down we go and join the action
with the dice and gaming faction.
What goes on inside the salon
where it's strictly cash per gallon
if you'd like to know, sir, well you
shut your mouth and I shall tell you.

Some are drinking, some are playing,
some their vulgar side displaying:
most of those who like to gamble
wind up naked in the scramble;
some emerge attired in new things,
some in bits and bobs and shoestrings:
no one thinks he'll kick the bucket
dicing for a beery ducat.

First to those who pay for wallowing,
then we layabouts toast the following:
next we drink to all held captive,
thirdly drink to those still active,
fourthly drink to the Christian-hearted,
fifthly drink to the dear departed,
sixthly to our free-and-easy sisters,
seventhly to all out-of-work enlisters.

Eighthly drink to friars deconverted,
ninthly, monks from monast'ries diverted,
tenthly, sailors of the oceans,
eleventhly, louts who cause commotions,
twelfthly, those who wear the penitential,
thirteenth, and whose journey is essential —
to this fat pope, to that thin king —
who the hell cares why they're drinking!

Drinking tinker, drinking tailor,
drinking soldier, drinking sailor,
drinking rich man, drinking poor man,
drinking beggarman, thief and lawman,
drinking servant, drinking master,
drinking mistress, drinking pastor,
drinking doctor, drinking layman,
drinking drunkard, drinking drayman:

Drinking rude man, drinking proper,
drinking tiddler, drinking whopper,
drinking scholar, drinking gypsy,
drinking drunk or maudlin tipsy,
drinking father, drinking mother,
drinking sister, drinking brother,
drinking husbands, wives and lovers
and a hundred thousand others —

Half a million pounds would never
pay for all we drink together:
for we drink beyond all measure,
purely for the sake of pleasure:
thus you see us, poor and shoddy,
criticized by everybody —
God grant that they be confounded
when at last the trump is sounded!

Amor volat undique
CB 87 (stanza 4, as edited by Schmeller)

> Love is flying all around
> with desire conjointly bound,
> young men and young women go
> fast entwined – and rightly so.
> But a girl without a mate
> undergoes a joyless fate,
> for her heart is locked up tight
> deep down inside
> frozen in an endless night . . .
> That's a most unhappy sight!

Dies, nox et omnia
CB 118 (stanzas 5, 6, 2)

Be it night or be it day
in my timeless disarray,
hearing maidens *bavarder*
  me fait complaindre –
and the more I sigh away
  plus me sens craindre.

Comrades, for a *jeu d'esprit*
summon your philosophy
and dispel my misery:
  grande douleur
bids you bend an ear to me
  pour votre honneur.

Of your face the loveliness
makes me weep, me weep *sans cesse* –
that you have a heart of ice:
  pour remédier,
you can bring me back to life
  par un baiser.

Stetit puella
CB 177   (stanzas 1, 2)

There was a girl who had
a tunic of bright red:
if anyone touched her
they'd set that dress astir!
  Aha!

She stood upon her toes
just like a little rose:
her face shone bright and fair,
and red lips blossomed there.
  Aha!

Circum mea pectora
CB 180   (stanzas 5, 6, 7)

Down inside the soul of me
sighs consume the whole of me
oh, for all your loveliness,
cause of all my heart's distress:

  *Lackaday, lackaday,
  will she never come my way?*

How the sparkling of your eyes
dims the sun that scours the skies! —
as the lightning streak that flings
brightness down on shadowed things.

May the gods of love be kind
to the plan I have in mind —
shatter to nihility
her chains of virginity.

Si puer cum puellula
CB 183   (as edited by Schmeller)

If ever boy and girl presume
to linger in a little room —
    happy their communion.

As yearning grows to burning
as yearning grows to burning
    equally within the two
they'll let their inhibitions go,
they lose their inhibitions — oh!
Into a thrilling game they fall
of lips and legs and limbs and all . . .

If ever boy and girl presume
to linger in a little room —
    happy their communion.

Veni, veni, venias
CB 174   (complete)

Come oh come oh come to me
or I die of misery!
Hyria, hyrie,
nazaza trillirivos!

Never saw a face so fair,
bright the eyes that sparkle there,
flowing waves of golden hair —
you're a picture past compare!

Redder than the rose's hue,
whiter than the lily's, too,
lovelier than all in view —
I will always worship you!

In trutina mentis dubia
From CB 70

In two minds one mind is seen to be
turning over helplessly:
  whether to favour
    Venus – or
      virginity.

But I'll choose as best I see,
bow my head, and willingly
  into the sweetest
    yoke of all
      surrender me.

Tempus est iocundum
CB 179   (stanzas 1, 4, 7, 5, 8)

Out you come – it's playtime
  you girls, again!
Join them in the May-time,
  young gentlemen!

  Oh, oh, oh,
  merrily we go!
  now I have a darling who
  has set my heart aglow:
  novel, novel, novel is the love
  that slays me oh! . . .

Promises you make me
  are ecstasy,
but when you forsake me
  they're agony!

In the winter season
  we're serious:
when the sap has risen,
  lascivious!

How can I have fun if
  I'm innocent?
How I am undone if
  I'm ignorant!

Come – with joy complying
  renew my love:
come along – I'm dying
  for you, my love!

Dulcissime
From CB 70

My darling love –
now I give you all I have . . .

Ave, formosissima
CB 77   (stanza 8)

Hail to thee, thou priceless gem,
  perfect and resplendent:
hail, thou pride of maidenhood,
  virgin most transcendent:
hail, thou Rose of all the World,
  Light all lights abasing:
Blanchefleur and Helen, thou –
  Venus all-embracing.

O Fortuna
CB 17   (reprise)

O how Fortune,
  inopportune,
apes the moon's inconstancy:
  waxing, waning,
  losing, gaining,
life treats us detestably:
  first oppressing
  then caressing
shifts us like pawns in her play:
  destitution,
  restitution,
mixes and melts them away.

Fate, as vicious
  as capricious,
whirling your merry-go-round:
  evil doings,
  worthless wooings,
crumble away to the ground:
  darkly stealing,
  unrevealing,
working against me you go:
  for your measure
  of foul pleasure
I bare my back to your blow.

Noble actions,
  true transactions,
no longer fall to my lot:
  powers to make me
  then to break me
all play their part in your plot:
  now seize your time —
  waste no more time,
pluck these poor strings and let go:
  since the strongest
  fall the longest
let the world share in my woe.

Appendix B
Notes

In the following notes, the abbreviations and references listed below are used. Where appropriate, a self-evident distinction is drawn between a *translation* and a *verse rendering*.

CB = (according to context) either the original manuscript known as *Codex Buranus*, or the 'critical' edition of *Carmina Burana* by Hilka, Schumann and Bischoff. CB followed by a number indicates the piece so numbered in Hilka–Schumann–Bischoff. If the number is asterisked the numbered piece forms part of the Supplement.

FB = *Fragmenta Burana*, as edited by Wilhelm Meyer. Its contents make up most of the Supplement.

Orff = the cantata *Carmina Burana* by Karl Orff (1937), based on the text of Schmeller (1847).

Raby = Latin text given in *The Oxford Book of Medieval Latin Verse* by F. J. E. Raby (1959).

Symonds = English verse renderings by A. J. Symonds in *Wine, Women and Song* (1894).

Waddell = English verse renderings by Helen Waddell in *Mediaeval Latin Lyrics* (1929, 1948); Waddell (WS) = her English verse renderings in *The Wandering Scholars* (1927, 1934).

Walsh = Latin texts edited and annotated by P. G. Walsh in *Thirty Poems from the Carmina Burana* (1976).

Whicher = American verse renderings by George F. Whicher in *The Goliard Poets* (1949).

CB 1   *Manus ferens munera*

Only the last four lines are preserved in the manuscript. The version in CB is reconstructed from several other manuscripts, none of which is

complete in itself; the most complete of these places the strophes in order
1, 4, 3, 2, 6.

The complaint against clerical corruption in general and simony in
particular is common enough. In this case it is conducted with verbal skill
of excruciating ingenuity, including puns and biblical resonances im-
possible to compact into verse translation. The last lines read: *Tale fedus
hodie / defedat et inficit / nostros ablativos, / qui absorbent vivos, / moti
per dativos / movent genitivos*, yielding a series of puns on the noun cases
ablative (literally 'taking away'), dative (literally 'giving'), and genitive
('possessing').

The verses are strictly trochaic throughout and rhyme a, b, a, b, a, b, c,
c, c, c.

Verse rendering also by Whicher.

CB2   *Responde, qui tanta cupis!*

Recorded in several manuscripts; author unknown. This conversation
between Plenty (*Copia*) and Avarice is expressed in hexameters which I
have merely hinted at in favour of a lightly colloquial rhythm.

CB3   *Ecce torpet probitas*

Ascribed to Walter of Châtillon; recorded in several manuscripts. Con-
tinues the theme of moral degeneracy with particular reference to avarice
and infidelity, but embraces a wider cross-section of society in its
strictures.

I have followed the rhyme scheme and trochaic rhythm as closely as
possible. The six-line stanzas are in goliardic measure rhyming a, b, a, b,
a, b, each followed by a three-line refrain rhyming c, d, c. The first line of
each refrain is *Omnes iura ledunt* (a touch of Delphic ambiguity?),
followed by a couplet more or less related to the topic of the preceding
stanza. I have, however, attached the refrain of stanza 5 (*Omnes iura
ledunt / et fidem in opere / quolibet excedunt*) to stanza 4, where it seems
more appropriate.

The grammatical word-play of stanza 3 (*Multum habet oneris / do –
das – dedi – dare*) is typical of the times: another example of the

personification of verbs may be found in CB 20, where we learn that *'Do das' et 'teneo' contendunt lite superba*.

In stanza 4, although Jupiter's infidelity to Juno was notorious, that of Dido to Aeneas is imaginary. I have resisted the temptation to return the boot to the proper foot.

Discussed and annotated in Walsh.

CB6   *Florebat olim studium*

Known only from CB. Curtius (*European Literature and the Latin Middle Ages*) takes this poem to illustrate the theme of 'the world upside down', quoting amongst other examples that of CB 37 in which 'cattle talk; the ox is harnessed behind the cart; capital and pedestal are interchanged; an ignorant fool becomes prior'. It will be noted that the references are biblical rather than classical.

I have arranged the fifty otherwise unseparated lines into four-line stanzas and followed the iambic tetrameters of the original: they make a welcome change from otherwise ubiquitous trochees.

Verse renderings by Whicher and (first fifteen lines) by Willard R. Trask in his translation of Curtius's work.

CB10   *Ecce sonat in aperto*

Only the first thirty-six lines appear in the manuscript: CB completes with fourteen lines recorded in two other sources.

A more bitter complaint about corruption in the Church, with simony repersonified. It is in rhyming couplets and trochaic rhythm, whose stiltedness when rendered closely in English seems for once to suit the somewhat fundamentalist tone of the sentiments expressed.

Verse rendering also by Whicher (incomplete).

CB16   *Fortune plango vulnera*

One of several songs on the fickleness of fate, and known only from CB. The image of Fortune spinning her wheel, simultaneously and apparently at random exalting some and abasing others, is of classical origin but reaches almost obsessive proportions in the later Middle Ages, as witnessed by the faulty placement of the miniature depicting Fortune's Wheel at the front of the manuscript in its present binding.

The hairy metaphor terminating stanza 1 has no counterpart in English, unless (as P. G. Walsh points out) in the desirability of 'seizing time by the forelock'. It may be traced to Cato, *Distychs*, 2, 26, 2, *fronte capillata, post est Occasio calvata*. Luck is seen as an approaching figure surmounted by a thick frontal chevelure hiding a thin, not to say balding, aftermath. One may liken the image to that of putting all the good fruit on top of the basket.

The verses are in irregular goliardic measure with internal rhyme. Of the consequent eight lines per stanza only the last four are unwaveringly trochaic. The rhyme scheme is basically a, b, a, b, c, d, c, d. I have followed this in English with alternate masculine and feminine rhymes, though the originals are a mixture of two- and three-syllabled rhymes of varying degrees of perfection.

Discussed and annotated in Walsh. Set by Orff.

CB 17   *O Fortuna*

Known only from CB, where it has been squeezed in beneath *Fas et nefas* on the same folio as the miniature of Fortune's Wheel. Like the preceding, this plaint on the fickleness of Fortune at her Wheel is subjective rather than general and may suggest an underlying personal experience.

The original is strictly trochaic. I follow the rhyme scheme and syllabic count exactly, but (under the influence of Orff's music) render the long lines as dactyls. The rhythm is identical with that of *Iste mundus* (CB 24), though the lines are differently arranged.

Set by Orff.

CB 19   *Fas et nefas*

Known from eight other manuscripts, with varying arrangements of stanzas.

The addressee of Walter's witty and scholastic begging poem is exhorted to the virtues of well-considered generosity rather than abandoned prodigality: 'Don't squander alms on riff-raff and so compromise your good name, but enhance your renown by seeking out and giving only to those most worthy of your honour – i.e., me.' For the concept of virtue as a midpoint between opposite vices, see also below. For another example of the genre, see CB 129, *Exul ego clericus*.

The reference to Codrus in the penultimate line is authentic (*cum sim Codro Codrior*) but not that to Croesus (*omnibus habundas*).

Annotated and discussed in Walsh. Verse rendering by Waddell (stanzas 1, 2, 3 only).

CB 20　*Est modus in verbis*

Four verses in hexameters present aspects of the view of virtue as the Golden Mean; that is, as the midpoint between opposite vices, for which an English equivalent might be found in the phrase 'Moderation in all things'.

Nos. I and II, recorded in other medieval manuscripts, are of unknown authorship; III is from Horace (*Epistles*, 1, 18, 9), also quoted by Ovid; IV is from Horace (*Satires*, 1, 2, 24), also quoted by Juvenal.

No. I is in rhyming couplets; II is in leonine hexameter (two lines with internal rhyme), which I have rewritten as four; III and IV are unrhymed.

CB 24　*Iste mundus*

The song is known from one other manuscript, its sentiment self-explanatory and redolent with biblical references.

The original is in thirteen strictly trochaic lines, all rhyming on the vowel *-a*, each line consisting of two rhymed diameters and a catalectic tetrameter.

> *Iste mundus　　furibundus　　falsa prestat gaudia . . .*

will be recognized as rhythmically identical with CB 17:

> *O Fortuna / velut luna / statu variabilis . . .*

Annotated and discussed by Walsh. Verse renderings by Whicher (in iambic rhythm, which I think loses impact) and Symonds.

CB28 *Laudat rite deum*

Ten moral aphorisms by Otloh of St Emmeram appear together in alphabetical order of (Latin) first words. Others by the same author occur elsewhere in this and other manuscripts.

Each saying is expressed in leonine hexameter, i.e. with half-line rhyming thus:

> *Laudat rite Deum   qui vere diligat illum.*

Attempts to match the hexameters in English produce particularly wordy results: in this case the gnomic nature of the text demands iambic pentameters, though I have matched the caesura and half-rhyme.

CB30 *Dum iuventus floruit*

One of three songs collectively headed *De conversione hominum* (CB29–31) and ascribed to Peter of Blois, expressing contrition for having led too worldly a life hitherto and vowing to lead a purer life henceforth. CB30 is a farewell to dissipation in general, CB29 more specifically to the erotic side of nature; both are known only from CB. CB31 continues the generality of CB30 but in a more tortuous and fragmented verse form, by comparison with which *Dum iuventus* sounds quite beguiling. It appears also (but incomplete) in FB and one other manuscript.

There is a very smooth verse rendering by Symonds, and another by Whicher, who takes greater liberties.

CB51a *Imperator rex Grecorum*

A crusading song relating to events which took place between the Second and Third Crusades. The Second, preached by St Bernard of Clairvaux in 1147, had miserably failed to preserve from Islamic pressure the states established by the First Crusade. Eventually Amalric I, King of Jerusalem, supported by the Byzantine Emperor Manuel Comnenus, made forays into Fatimid Egypt and in 1168 succeeded in rendering it tributary. Unfortunately for him, the young general Saladin, sent to aid the Egyp-

tians, himself seized power and became Sultan of Egypt and Syria – two
countries separated by the Kingdom of Jerusalem. Saladin's capture of
Jerusalem in 1187 prompted the Third Crusade.

The four stanzas, each monorhymed, are in strict trochees. The refrain
is a corrupt version of the Trisagion (or Tersanctus, 'thrice holy'), an
ancient hymn invoking divine mercy in alternate Greek and Latin lines.
The immediately preceding piece – CB 51, *Debacchatur mundus pomo* –
is a plaint on the sins of the world. Though not thematically related to
CB 51a, it is formally identical, and the two appear without a break in the
original manuscript.

CB 54   *Omne genus demoniorum*

An incantation, known only from CB. I have adhered more closely to the
rhythms and rhyme scheme of the original, with turgid results by
comparison with Helen Waddell's looser, shorter and more fluent verse
rendering. Turgidity, however, may not be out of place in a piece of this
nature.

CB 62   *Dum Diane vitrea*

This haunting nocturne is recorded only in CB and remains anonymous
despite several attempts at ascription to various poets of the time
(including Peter Abélard).

Of irregular format, it falls into three parts. Stanzas 1 to 4 evoke
nocturnal landscapes and welcome sleep as a soothing relief from every-
day troubles. Stanzas 5 and 6 follow two further lines of thought: first,
the pleasurable alternation of sleep and love-making; second, in ana-
tomical vein, the effects of sleep upon the body. Stanzas 7 and 8 pursue
the theme of love from immediate pleasures to the outer reaches of
generality.

Schumann, editing this part of the critical edition, considered the
original piece to consist only of stanzas 1 to 4, and relegated to the fine
print of footnotes stanzas 5 to 8 as an irrelevant accretion to a song which
is primarily about sleep and hardly concerns itself with love. He even
casts doubt on the authenticity of the two references to love in stanzas 1

to 4. Many agree with Schumann; but dissension from his view is strenuously argued by Peter Dronke in *Medieval Latin and the Rise of European Love-Lyric*.

(In this connection it is tempting to take into account that the parody of *Dum Diane* represented by CB 197, *Dum domus lapidea*, itself extends further than four stanzas. Besides being inept, however, the parody is incomplete, and after the fourth stanza the parodist seems to lose touch with his model.)

I have attempted a rendering of the entire manuscript version (stanzas 1 to 8) for the sake of completeness. This entails inevitable assumptions about the intention of the whole, which consequently bear on the interpretation of stanzas 1 to 4 alone. For example, the end of the first stanza reads: *sic emollit / vis chordarum pectora / et immutat / cor, quod nutat / ad amoris pignora*. Apart from doubts cast on the original authenticity of any reference to love, the lines seem open to conflicting interpretations. The 'music', be it of zephyrs, lutes or spheres, either affects the heart so that it turns to love as a natural activity for the time of evening, or lures to the pleasures of sleep such hearts as were already so inclined and thus need to be turned *from* that preoccupation. Which line to take depends on whether one regards the whole poem as stanzas 1 to 8 on the subject of sleep and love, or as stanzas 1 to 4 on the subject of sleep alone. The MS *pignora* ('pledges') is consistent with the emphasis on love, but Schumann and other critics here assume scribal error for *pondera* ('burdens'), which would favour the interpretive preference for sleep.

Other parts of the text require elucidation or are the subject of debate. Diana's lantern is of course the moon, and her brother is the sun (Apollo), whose light from low on the horizon pinkly tints the underside of the lunar lamp (the operative word is *succenditur*, 'is lit from below'). *Sero* ('late') and Hesperus (the evening star) suggest evening, but it has been pointed out that reference to dew suggests morning, for which purpose the sun could as well be rising as setting. The first line of stanza 4 sees a tussle between 'Orpheus' in manuscript and Schumann's emendation to 'Morpheus'.

Stanza 6 begins *Ex alvo leta fumus evaporat / qui capitis tres cellulos irrorat*. In medieval anatomy, following Albertus Magnus, the brain was regarded as consisting of three connected chambers. A more exact translation would refer to 'the three-celled brain', or words to that effect.

Stanza 8 ends *Fluctuat inter spem metumque dubia / sic Veneris militia*: an explicit reference to the common image of love as quasi-military service to Venus. Its mood certainly seems a long way removed from the magic of the opening.

The metre is irregular and there is scope for differences of opinion as to the scansion in several places, but I have reproduced the metrics and rhyme scheme quite closely.

Symonds renders the whole poem, but in rhyming couplets of equal length and metre (that of the opening lines) throughout. Much seems lost in the resultant symmetry. Whicher restricts himself to the first four stanzas; Waddell omits stanzas 6 and 8. Latin, translation and discussion of whole (stanzas 1 to 8) by Dronke (*op. cit.*). Latin and discussion in Walsh, Robertson (*Essays in Medieval Culture*), Jackson (*The Interpretation of Medieval Latin Poetry*), Waddell (W.S.).

CB66 *Acteon, Lampos*

Known from one other manuscript. Written in leonine hexameter. The subjects are personifications of the four horses who successively draw Apollo's chariot across the sky during the course of the day.

CB70 *Estatis florigero tempore*

This beautiful poem, known only from CB, looks at first sight to be a straightforward seduction scene like CB72, *Grates ago Veneri*. It opens with a typical 'nature introduction' establishing summer as the seasonal background (*sibilante serotino frigore* seems contradictory, and Schumann suggests, if not scribal error, 'a light breeze, precursor of the wintry season'; I have taken it to be the sort of cooling breeze that blows later in the afternoon and passes inexorably to 'thoughts of love' expressed from the viewpoint of the first person, male. One might be led to expect a dreary rape scene. Instead, the poet diverges into the path of dialogue between the two principals, in which 'he' pleads and argues, and 'she' resists, argues, and eventually yields. One feels that she gets the better of the argument, and that the outcome consummates not so much a seduction on his part as a gift, an act of generosity, on hers.

Such, of course, is part of the courtly love tradition. Indeed, *Estatis florigero* may appear as full of conventions as *Hamlet* is of quotations: the nature introduction, the appeal to Venus, the metaphor of desire as a flame to be quenched or a pain to be cured by its object, the reference to brotherly solicitude (compare 'big brother Martin' in CB 158), the 'courtly' notion of concealing the lady's identity and protecting her from rumour (see also CB 77, stanza 2, and CB 111, stanza 2). Yet it strikes me as sincerely personal and quite sensitive in its unusual expression of interest in the woman's viewpoint. I find it more appealing than CB 77, *Si linguis angelicis*, which has come in for inordinate praise.

The poem is apparently incomplete – the transition from stanza 2 to stanza 3 is somewhat abrupt, suggesting that other courses of action might have been considered and abandoned in a missing stanza – and poses some problems of interpretation, particularly in determining who says what in the lines which I present here as the girl's first speech.

It takes the form of a sequence, with the dialogue expressed in matching pairs of stanzas. Except in the first few lines, I have followed the metrics and rhyme scheme closely. The opening lines form a fascinating metrical ascent which I cannot reproduce in English without loss of fluency:

> *Estátis florígero témpore*
> *sub úmbrosa résidens aŕbore,*
> *ávibus canéntibus in némore,*
> *síbilante sérotino frígore,*
> *mée Thísbes ádoptáto frúebár elóquió,*
> *cólloquéns de Vénerís blandíssimo commérció.*

The couplets are respectively in triple, quadruple and duple rhythm, and of increasing length.

The piece is briefly discussed by Dronke in *Medieval Latin and the Rise of European Love-Lyric*, p. 255.

CB 71   *Grates ago Veneri*

Another seduction scene, and known from one other manuscript, *Grates ago* contrasts strikingly with *Estatis florigero*. The poet (Peter of Blois) does not waste time with the flowers that bloom in the spring but states from the outset that he has had his way and then proceeds to offer a blow-by-blow account of the way in which he has had it. His partner's thoughts and feelings on the encounter are left to the imagination, unless we seriously believe that 'she enjoyed it in the end and therefore really wanted it all the time'. Whether she succumbs through 'generosity', that courtly quality leading to the consummation of CB70, or through sheer exhaustion, seems at best arguable.

Two literary conventions are worthy of note: that of passionate pursuit as military service on behalf of Venus (as in CB62, which in the Latin ends *sic Veneris militia*), and that of the 'five stages' of love outlined in stanza 3 (or more accurately stanza 2a, since the poem takes the form of a strict sequence):

> *Visu, colloquio,*
> *contactu, basio*
> *frui virgo dederat . . .*

She had, he says, permitted the first four stages of looking, speaking, touching and kissing – now only the fifth remains to be realized.

The subtlety of language and ingeniousness of rhyme schemes (which I have paralleled fairly accurately) contrast strangely with the forthrightness of expression. This may partly explain why I do not really feel the poet/persona to be as male chauvinist as I have suggested above – though I do not think I would go so far as to endorse Peter Dronke's assessment of the poem as 'a radiantly joyful description of how the lover wins his lass' (*Medieval Latin and the Rise of European Love-Lyric*). One may rather detect an element of literary braggadocio about the whole affair.

CB75 *Omittamus studia*

Known only from CB. The subject invites comparison with CB216, *Tempus hoc letitie*, but is deeper in argument, emotion and expression. Otherwise, it may be left to speak for itself. The last couplet of stanza 1 is missing from the manuscript, and I have based my rendering on lines supplied by Herkenrath (quoted in CB): *res est apta senectuti / seriis intendere, / res est apta iuventuti / leta mente ludere.*

Verse renderings by Symonds (smooth, and faithful to text and metre), Waddell (wandering, with somewhat fey results), Whicher (spoils the metre); discussed and annotated by Walsh.

CB77 *Si linguis angelicis*

This puzzling poem, of unknown authorship and recorded only in CB, looks at first sight like another tale of successful wooing recounted from the poet's masculine viewpoint. It has its fair share of appropriate literary conceits and conventions: biblical imagery, classical references, notions of courtly love, thinly disguised parody and many more. But it tends to take unexpected turns which may leave the modern reader in the surrealistic dilemma of uncertainty as to the ultimate intent.

The expected nature opening is abandoned in favour of New Testament imagery. The first line of stanza 1, 'Though I speak with the tongues of men and of angels' (I Corinthians 13, 1), needs no explanation. That of stanza 2 is the opening of a sixth-century Easter hymn by Venantius Fortunatus. It was often borrowed for other hymns, such as that which appears as CB20*: *Pange, lingua, gloriose / virginis martyrium . . .* , 'Praise, O tongue, the martyrdom of the glorious Virgin.'

Thus the poet uses the Christian imagery of divine love to express his spiritual elation at the 'palm' or prize he has won by (as we shall discover) the yielding of his beloved. He then promptly turns to the courtly love tradition by asserting the need for discretion in the matter of identity. To this topic, also evidenced in CB70 and CB111, the classic reference is Andreas Capellanus, *The Art of Courtly Love*, II, 1: 'The man who wants to keep his love affair untroubled should above all things be careful not to let it be known to any outsider, but should keep it hidden from everybody . . .'

A third abrupt turn brings him, and us, to a flower-garden, where the subsequent action takes place. This is not to be regarded as a delayed 'nature introduction'. The formal garden is a common medieval metaphor for a mood or state of mind: Guillaume de Lorris may already have been at work on *Le Roman de la Rose* when the CB manuscript was being compiled. The setting now gives us a choice of pegs on which to hang our reading of the story. It may be literally true (allowing for some degree of poetic licence); it may be a purely imaginative transformation of a real occurrence; or it may be an elaborate exercise in wishful thinking executed with a problematical degree of sincerity.

The poet wonders whether he is getting anywhere in his aspirations towards the girl he loves, or whether his advances are like the seed that falls by the wayside or on stony ground in the parable of the sower. The chief stumbling-block seems to be an old woman, a duenna, who carefully shields his 'Rose' from either giving or receiving the gift of love. Cursing the hag, and calling upon Pluto to rise from the underworld and snatch her away – or, better still, thunderbolt her out of existence – he suddenly finds his wish granted, the crone gone for good (we hear no more of her), and his Rose in all her loveliness awaiting him in the garden.

He greets her with rare effusion (*Ave, formosissima*), likening her in turn to precious stones and the Holy Virgin, subsequently to Blanchefleur, Helen, and Venus. Blanchefleur being the heroine of the medieval romance *Floire and Blanchefleur*, the beloved is thus related to ideals of womanhood from every operative culture of the time: Christian, Greek, Roman and – in the poet's eyes – modern European. (At least two of these figures, it may be observed for future reference, are not noted for their virginity.)

By yet another abrupt change of tone, the girl returns his greeting in a manner refreshingly simple and literally down to earth – 'May God, who made the world with violets studding the grass and thorns inseparable from roses, keep you well, sir!' Knowing the eventual outcome, we may again be reminded of lines from Andreas Capellanus: from the Eighth Dialogue, 'The solaces of love are medicines which purge away all griefs and restore all joys . . .'; and from the Second, 'May God give you a reward suited to your effort.' The reference to thorns accompanying roses is not without point, and the wish for 'good health' to the aspirant introduces a long passage in which the poet, in typically medieval metaphor, expounds his suffering in more or less medical terms. 'Only you can cure it!' echoes the plea of CB70, amongst others of its time. (The metaphor of the shipwreck, which appears later, is not uncommon: it occurs twice in Andreas and elsewhere in CB.)

Having finished his recital and thrown himself on her mercy, the lover – who has been quietly yearning for her for the best part of six years without making any progress – is astonished to discover that she has been no less hopelessly enamoured of him for (presumably) the same length of time.

Instead of yielding immediately, which would abrupt the adventure to excess, the Rose, either artfully or ingenuously, sets the encounter off on another tack. She is only too anxious to satisfy his needs, but is apparently uncertain as to what he has in mind. Gold – silver – jewels, perhaps? These may be beyond her, but she will gladly do her best. 'This is not what I had in mind,' he is forced by honesty to admit, and seeks to put her right by means of a conundrum: 'That which means more to me than riches, is much healthier . . .' and so on. (*Cf.* Andreas, Seventh Dialogue: 'I desire Your Clemency to be informed that the reward I ask you to promise to give me is one which it is unbearable agony to be without, while to have it is to abound in all riches . . . It is your love which I seek, in order to restore my health.') Again she professes ignorance, and can do no more to prove her desire to accommodate him than to invite him to take from her whatever he can find of interest to his condition. She does not actually say

'Seek, and you shall find; knock, and it shall be opened unto you', but that sentiment may well spring to mind.

So, at last, they come together. The poet reverts to his opening image of the 'palm' he has won, and rounds the piece off with a moral: things are never as black as they seem: if you want something badly enough it will eventually come to you.

The poem puzzles largely because of its abrupt turns and anticlimaxes. Are they intended for humorous effect, or do they reflect the poet's vacillating moods and nodes of indecision? Are the biblical references and parallels to be interpreted as parodies for the purpose of raising a knowing smile on the part of the reader/audience, or is the poet gripped by so ecstatic a response to his taste of love that ordinary words fail him and only the divine will do? These extremes of interpretation are represented respectively by D. W. Robertson jun. (*Essays in Medieval Culture*), who treats the whole thing as an academic joke, and Peter Dronke (*Medieval Latin and the Rise of European Love-Lyric*), who describes it as 'a love vision that foreshadows the *Roman de la Rose*' and (albeit 'tentatively') as 'an emblem of the twelfth- and thirteenth-century European poetry of *amour courtois*'.

Robertson's argument depends largely on examples of what he sees as deliberate bathos for humorous effect. In each of the first two stanzas, for instance, the first couplet appears to herald a purely religious experience which is promptly contradicted by the down-to-earth nature of the second. In the *Ave, formosissima* section he points to a moral descent in the catalogue of womanly ideals from the Holy Virgin to Venus via Blanchefleur and Helen. Helen's reputation, we are reminded, was at a low stock in the Middle Ages. To liken his beloved first to the paragon of maidenhood and progressively down to pagan sex symbols is hardly as flattering as the poet pretends. Dronke averts this problem by urging, for example, that 'Helen signifies the true, innocent Helen of Egypt, whose story was known through Servius'. Certainly there are discrepancies in tone between the carnal and the spiritual, but their purpose is to elevate the former to the status of the latter. If true love is divine, its consummation approaches the sacramental.

The two positions seem somewhat extreme and not entirely mutually exclusive. From these and other essays Robertson seems as blind to the paradoxical realities of love as Dronke does to the legitimacy of humour as means to a serious end. I do find the expression humorous, but am in no doubt as to the sincerity of the emotion. The puzzlement of the poem may be seen as reflecting that of a young man who has undergone an ecstatic experience and expresses an inability to cope with it by alternating self-consciously between euphuism and flippancy. Alternatively, it might be regarded as pure fantasy based on wishful thinking. We are discouraged by critics from applying modern concepts and criteria to pre-modern texts, but how are we to respond to any text other than according to our own lights and experience? One might, therefore, dare to suggest that the poet is indeed in love, and has been for some time, but through inexperience or inadequacy has failed to make the proper advances. The hag guarding his Rose – a crone of thorns, as it were – unconsciously represents his own inhibitions. Only in the realm of daydream does he find the courage to cast them off and say the beautiful things to her that all lovers imagine before an encounter but are unable to articulate when the time comes. Only in daydreams do objects 'of many years' adoring' confess to reciprocal yearnings of equally long standing, and only in daydreams do they tease so transparently before yielding so unconditionally.

There is a verse rendering by Whicher, fairly neutral in tone but ending, with a flourish, in the rhyming of *bee-stings* with *feastings*. Symonds refers but briefly to CB77 and translates two stanzas. The Orff cantata includes a setting of *Ave, formosissima*.

(NOTE The first line of the last stanza was originally written in manuscript *Ex amara equidem generantur*, 'Out of bitterness [something plural omitted] are born.' A later hand has completed the line by adding *amara* before *generantur*; 'Out of bitterness are bitternesses born.' Schumann corrects *amara* to *grata*, 'pleasurable things', which is clearly in keeping with the rest of the stanza and indeed with the tenor of the whole piece. Robertson seeks to retain *amara*, seeing it as the poet's final admission of insincerity: an acknowledgement that the whole thing was a wishful dream and that he is not really any better off than he was before. It seems worth pointing out that *amara*, even if it were apt, would prove the only example of faulty scansion – a trochee is required – in a total of 132 lines.)

CB85 *Veris dulcis in tempore*

This delicate song occurs twice in CB (Nos. 85 and 159) and is known also from a Catalan manuscript with a variant stanza 4.

Unlike many girls' names encountered hitherto, Juliana is not classical and appears nowhere else in CB, though I think she should be taken as a universal rather than a particular. Some observations by Ernest Weekley may be relevant here. 'Gillian is the popular form of Juliana, which, for some unknown reason, was a favourite medieval font-name. Like most female names in common use it acquired a derogatory sense and became equivalent to wench, light o' love, etc. Gillian-flirt and Gill-flirt were common terms of reproach from the 16th century onward . . .' (*Words and Names*, 1932, p. 82)

Verse renderings by Symonds, Whicher. The latter seems to regard Juliana as a particular.

CB 87   *Amor tenet omnia*

A rhyming catalogue of all love's paradoxes: it (or rather he, as Amor is an alias of Cupid) is warm but cool, modest but shameless, courageous but cowardly, and so on. The song is known only from CB, in which it is described by Schumann as one of the most corruptly transmitted of the collection and perhaps the most problematical to interpret. Even the order of stanzas is open to argument, different commentators following different arrangements. I have followed Schumann's version closely, both in sense and in form.

The same arrangement is followed by Symonds in his verse rendering. Orff sets one stanza, the fourth (*Amor volat undique*), following the edition and interpretation of J. A. Schmeller.

CB 90   *Exiit diluculo*

This anonymous song seems to be an incomplete pastourelle with a spurious ending. The first eight lines are known from CB and one other manuscript. The last four appear only in CB and give the impression of having been added as a crude rounding-off.

Viewing this lightweight, though delightful, piece as a welcome passage of comic relief at a point in the collection much in need of it, I have taken the liberty of changing trochees to anapaests, which strike me as more in keeping with the spirit of the original.

The version by Symonds is iambic and comparatively staid; that of Whicher abandons all regularity of metre and reads like a string of clerihews. Latin to be found in Raby.

CB 92   *Anni parte florida*
('Phyllis and Flora')

The famous debate between Phyllis and Flora as to the relative merits of knight and cleric as lover is known from a dozen or so medieval manuscripts, attesting to its widespread popularity. No version is complete in itself, that of the CB manuscript breaking off in the middle of stanza 62 through loss of folios prior to binding. The author is unknown; an Italian provenance is suggested.

Rivalry in love between knight and cleric is a common literary theme of the twelfth and thirteenth centuries both in Latin and the emergent vernaculars. That the cleric usually wins (an exception is provided in *Floire et Blanchefleur*), besides being a foregone conclusion in view of the obvious authorship, is an interesting reflection on the need of the rapidly expanding educated classes to assert their social standing in a world hitherto dominated by the military, if not chivalric, ideal. As Walsh points out (*Thirty Poems from the Carmina Burana*), celibacy was at this period expected only of those who performed the sacramental liturgy; marriage was 'not out of the question' for simple clerics who wore the habit and tonsure but had not been admitted to minor orders.

Phyllis, champion of the knight, and Flora, enamoured of the cleric, are popular characters in medieval literature (they also appear in CB 59, *Ecce, chorus virginum*). Both names are suggestive of spring, Flora the Roman goddess of flowers, Phyllis deriving from the Greek for 'leaf'.

The poem falls into four parts. Part 1 (stanzas 1–11) sets the scene, with a nature introduction, an account of the girls' beauty and nobility, and the establishment of a *locus amoenus* or 'pleasance' in which the debate is to take place. A parallel may be found, as usual, in Andreas Capellanus, *The Art of Courtly Love* (in this case one of equal relevance to CB 70, *Estatis florigero*): in the Seventh Dialogue, the couple identified as 'the woman A. and Count G.' seek an arbitrator's decision from the Countess of Champagne in a letter beginning: 'Now on a certain day, as we sat under the shade of a pine tree of marvellous height and great breadth of spread, devoted wholly to Love's idleness and striving to investigate Love's mandates in a good-tempered and spirited debate . . .'

Part 2 (stanzas 12–43) relates the arguments between the girls as to the pros and cons of the men in question. The exchanges alternate with increasing rapidity and apparent even-handedness, though the cleric may already be observed to receive a greater proportion of actual lines. Many of the sentiments are common currency, and again may be illustrated from Andreas. In Chapter VII we read that 'the life of the clergy is, because of the continual idleness and the great abundance of food, naturally more liable to temptations of the body than that of any other men'; and in the Eighth Dialogue 'a clerk comes before us dressed in women's clothes, unsightly because of his shaven head ... given up to continual indolence and devoted only to his belly.' In the last two stanzas, Phyllis and Flora agree to take their dispute to arbitration at the court of Cupid, god of love. At this point reality, if such it was, starts to dissolve into fantasy.

Part 3 (stanzas 44–59) may be described as an intermezzo in which the transformation from reality to fantasy is completed. It will have been observed that all cultural references hitherto have been classical, with not a hint of Christian or biblical imagery. We now enter a long passage extolling the virtues and tracing the pedigree of the creatures on which Phyllis and Flora propose to effect their journey, from which it appears that practically the whole Roman pantheon has been unwittingly involved.

Part 4 (stanzas 60–79) sees their rapid arrival at the groves where Cupid holds court and an effusive description of the everyday musical proceedings with which the cherubic god is habitually regaled. They explain their quest, and, with just three stanzas to spare, the problem is put before a closed session of their host's court. The answer comes out, like clockwork, in favour of the cleric. Everybody approves the decision and resolves to hold it binding for ever – with the possible exception of Phyllis, from whom, unfortunately, as from her happier companion, we hear not another word. Possibly, too, with the exception of Cupid. That he could not be bothered to answer the question personally may reflect on the traditional blindness of love – on Cupid's habit of loosing darts off hither and thither as the fancy takes him. One target is as good as another: he is no respecter of persons, either as individuals or as types.

The whole is in goliardic measure: each four-lined stanza is monorhymed and scans in strict trochees with an invariable caesura. In English I have recast in eight lines with two pairs of rhymes and in most cases have admitted an extra unstressed syllable between original half-lines. I know of no other complete verse rendering in modern English. Symonds offers the first twelve stanzas and the fourteen which embody description of Cupid's court, cleverly (but with inevitable loss of fluency) reproducing the strict trochees and four rhymes per stanza of the original.

(An English translation was first published in 1595 under the title *The Amorous Contention of Phillis and Flora* in George Chapman's *Ouid's*

Banquet of Sence . . . With a translation of a Latin coppie, written by a Fryer, Anno Dom. 1400; and again in 1598 under the title *Phillis and Flora. The sweete and ciuill contention of two amorous Ladyes. Translated out of Latine, by R. S. Esquire.* 'R. S.', according to the *Dictionary of National Biography*, could have been Chapman's friend Richard Stapleton.)

Discussed and annotated by Walsh.

CB 95   *Cur suspectum me tenet domina?*

Known only from CB: a gloomy song – the first in a series of varied love complaints – whose singer, portrayed as a scholar studying abroad, defends himself against his lady's accusation of homosexuality. The homeland to which he refers appears in manuscript as *Briciauuia*, which has been taken as a corrupt rendering of *Britannia*.

While retaining the four rhymes per stanza of the original, I have turned the decasyllabic lines into straightforward iambs. The original lines in fact follow the same interesting metrical pattern as CB 119, *Dulce solum*, namely two half-lines consisting respectively of two trochees and three iambs.

Latin in Raby.

CB 111   *O comes amoris dolor*

This anonymous love complaint is known only from CB, where it appears twice: once in the body of the codex (CB 111), stanzas 1 and 4 only, and again in *Fragmenta* (supplemental CB 8*). The order of stanzas followed here is that of Schumann – in FB it is 1, 3, 4, 2.

Given (as I believe) the correctness of Schumann's rearrangement, the poet uses elements of courtly love and other literary conventions to rare effect. The usual pattern of a nature introduction leading to appropriate (or contrasting) thoughts of love, a passage from the general to the particular, is here reversed. He opens, instead, by focusing on the point of his concern – 'sorrow, love's inseparable companion' – then pulls away to reveal the woman who is the cause of his sorrow, and yet further away to the valley which is her home. This progression illustrates the theme of exile expressed in the opening, which might otherwise have passed as a commonplace. He finally achieves 'solace' (normally a courtly code-word for consummation) in contemplation of that valley which is beautified by its intimate association with the beloved. Nature ceases to be an introduction, either impartial or disturbing; instead, it is transformed into a healing conclusion.

Of particular 'courtly' interest are the higher social status of the beloved and the consequently greater need for secrecy as to her identity.

There are verse renderings of stanzas 1 and 4 by Symonds and Waddell. Whicher rejects Schumann's ordering of stanzas and retains that of FB as edited by Meyer. Entitling his version *Sally in her Alley* and commenting on Waddell's romantic leanings, he argues that it 'falls over into comedy somewhat akin to the seventeenth-century song of *Phillida flouts me*'. One can only take comfort from the fact that the author of *O comes* was probably unacquainted with Whicher's model.

Discussed and annotated in Walsh; Latin also in Raby. Both accept Schumann's arrangement and readings.

CB114   *Tempus accedit floridum*

Known only from CB, this is a typical lover's complaint with conventional nature introduction, praise of the beloved, expression of grief and the certainty that only she can cure his malady. One mark of distinction is the employment of iambic rhythm throughout.

The order of strophes in the manuscript is 2, 3, 4, 1: I follow Schumann's rearrangement, and he in turn follows Bojunga. (*Tempus accedit floridum* is an almost standard opening line: four other songs follow the same pattern in CB alone.) Each consists of six lines rhyming a, b, a, b, c, c, but the last consists of two half-lines which I have split into two with a third appearance of the rhyme. The final couplet of stanza 4 – *o tu mitis considera! / nam pro te gemitus   passus sum et suspiria* – appears spurious and lacks two syllables.

Verse rendering by Waddell, who follows CB order (beginning *Prata iam rident omnia*). Discussed and annotated by Walsh.

CB116   *Sic mea fata canendo solor*

Known from three manuscripts, one of which, written as prose, is also from Benediktbeuern. Only the prose version includes stanza 3.

The series of lovers' complaints continues with the pathetic song of one who is too old to attract the favours of the girl by whom he is smitten. Its unusual lyricism is largely ascribable to the dactylic rhythm – it is written, so to speak, in triple time – and striking repetitions.

Stanza 3, not found in the *Codex Buranus* itself, is rejected by Schumann as an 'over the top, over-explicit and gratuitous accretion' (*ubersteigende, verdeutlichende, vergrobernde Zudichtung*) on grounds of both style and content. This strikes me as fair comment: I include the stanza for the sake of completeness.

Verse renderings by Symonds, Waddell, Whicher, all of three stanzas. Latin in Raby, two only. The third, as edited by Schumann, reads:

> *Ubera cum animadverterem,*
> *optavi, manus ut involverem,*
> *simplicibus mammis ut alluderem.*
> *Sic cogitando traxi Venerem;*
> *sedit in ore*
> *rosa cum pudore,*
> *pulsatus amore*
> *quod os lamberem,*
> *hei lamberem! hei lamberem! hei lamberem!*
> *luxuriando per characterem!*

CB 118   *Doleo, quod nimium*

This love complaint, known only from CB, basically expresses the fears of a student in France that his girl-friend at home (in Germany?) may be diverting her affection to someone more immediately accessible – though parts of it are not entirely consistent with the theme. Appropriately macaronic, with French as the second language, it is corruptly transmitted and poses problems of reading and interpretation extensively discussed by Schumann. The inconsistent parts, particularly stanza 2 and the first four lines of stanza 7, may belong to another piece, and Hilka argued for the rejection of stanza 4.

I have followed Schumann's text as closely as possible, using Hilka's suggested reading *po dura, laissa iadis* for the questionable *podyra mi lassa dis* in stanza 4.

Orff sets stanzas 5, 6, 2 (*Dies, nox et omnia*).

CB 119   *Dulce solum natalis patrie*

In many ways CB 119, recorded in different versions in six manuscripts, forms a contrasting companion piece to CB 118, above. The singer, about to travel abroad – to study in France, perhaps? – bids farewell to home, friends and native country in terms which bring to mind Welsh songs expressive of *hiraeth*. (Line 1 immediately suggests 'Land of my Fathers' and the continuation finds a parallel in Llew Tegid's *'Ffarwel i Walia'*:

> *Ffarwel i'r fwthyn fy mam a nhad,*
> *ffarwel, gyfoedion bob un . . .*

'Farewell to my parents' cottage; goodbye, companions each and every one . . .')

He also laments the sorrows of love, though their exact circumstances are unclear: it may be that an unhappy love affair is driving him away, or that he is forced away by external pressures and fears the sort of consequence illustrated in CB 116 – or, indeed, that he has himself struggled between love and vocation and regretfully chosen the latter.

I have here translated the version as edited by Schumann. In manuscript it contains five stanzas, each of which is followed by a (different) one-word 'refrain' echoing the mood of the preceding lines. All other sources agree, however, in exhibiting only four stanzas, while CB's fifth not only is corrupt but also, as Schumann points out, breaks the pattern of the other stanzas by merely repeating in other words the sentiments of the one before. The one-word tailpieces, though also appearing in a manuscript from Chartres, are of debatable suitability. (They may have been added by a particular performer on a particular occasion.) The order of stanzas in CB is 1, 2, 4, 3, followed by the supernumerary. Schumann's order, followed here, is that of the Chartres manuscript and strikes me as self-evidently appropriate.

The lines are decasyllabic but follow the distinctive pattern of two half-lines containing respectively two trochees and three iambs (as also in CB 95).

For an English rendering of the full version see Symonds, who follows the manuscript order of five stanzas but, curiously, turns the lines into alexandrines (six iambs each). Discussed and annotated by Walsh; Latin also in Raby: both of four stanzas only and omitting the one-word appendages.

CB 126 *Huc usque, me miseram!*

Further variety is introduced into the sequence of love complaints by this rare and sensitive assumption of the woman's viewpoint of a circumstance less commonly encountered in medieval poetry than, no doubt, in real life: that of unintended pregnancy. The girl's acceptance of and excuse for the perhaps unsurprising disappearance of her lover is expressed with touching irony.

The song is known only from CB. In manuscript it consists of fourteen three-line stanzas of which the first reads as follows, including a refrain:

> *Tempus instat floridum,*
> *cantus crescit avium,*
> *tellus dat solacium.*
> > *Eya,*
> > *qualia*
> > *sunt amoris gaudia!*

The mood of this opening (spring flowers, bird-song, pleasing countryside, such are love's delights) is clearly at variance with the subject and on these grounds it is rejected by most commentators. Some assert, and I must say I agree, that on purely internal grounds the opening stanza could intentionally establish a background to the action of the song which contrasts with it ('Most people are out enjoying themselves – but not I'), while the refrain increases in irony throughout: 'Such are love's (socalled) delights in stark reality.' I am, however, swayed to their exclusion by the likelier suggestion that the said lines constitute yet another example of an opening without its true continuation. There are several such instances in CB, and many songs of similar opening mood, but no comparable examples of such irony.

Some also reject the penultimate stanza and print the remainder as three twelve-line stanzas in various arrangements. I retain short stanzas as being appropriate to the theme and tone of the song.

Verse renderings by Symonds (omitting stanzas 1 and 13 and recasting as three twelve-line stanzas) and Whicher (accepting stanza 1 as an introduction and following other arrangements). Discussed and annotated by Walsh; Latin also in Raby: both reject the introductory piece.

CB 129   *Exul ego clericus*

An anonymous begging song known only from CB (cf. CB 19), designed
for universal applicability by the *ad hoc* incorporation of a prospective
patron's name. (Stanza 5 begins *Decus N—*.)

Verse renderings by Symonds ('I have tried to follow the sing-song
doggerel') and Whicher; discussed and annotated by Walsh.

CB 130   *Olim lacus colueram*

The song of the roast swan, known only from CB, appropriately termin-
ates this sequence of complaints – hardly a love complaint, except in so
far as the poor thing (though not a raw thing) must have been much in
love with life. Roast swan was a greatly appreciated delicacy amongst
those who could afford it, and pepper a comparatively recent import
(stanza 4: *Mallem in aquis vivere, / nudo semper sub aere, / quam in hoc
mergi pipere*). Medieval cooks relied heavily on spices and flavourings for
culinary effect, partly as relief from the limited range of foods available,
partly to disguise the taste of food of dubious origin or excessive storage
time – especially in the case of meat during the winter. An additional
point of interest is made by Fernand Braudel in *The Structures of
Everyday Life*: 'Every civilization needs dietary luxuries and stimulants.
In the twelfth and thirteenth centuries the craze was for spices and
pepper; then it was tea and coffee, not to mention tobacco.'

I have followed the syllabic count, rhyming pattern and iambic rhythm
exactly, accepting Schumann's placement in second position of the stanza
appearing fourth in the manuscript, and following Laistner's arrange-
ment of lines in stanza 3 (which differs both from the manuscript and
Schumann).

Verse renderings by Symonds and Whicher, following manuscript
order (thus unwittingly justifying Schumann's rearrangement). Set, ex-
cruciatingly, by Orff.

CB 136   *Omnia sol temperat*

Anonymous; known only from CB; followed by German-language piece
(CB 136a, *Solde ih noch den tach geleben*).

The sorrows of love and other complaints are followed by a number of spring songs reverting to its joys, of which *Omnia sol* is typical (not least in being followed by a German strophe singable to the same melody, though not necessarily expressing the same mood or argument). Where previous songs bemoan actual breaches between students travelling abroad and the girls they have left behind, this affirms the singer's fidelity and expresses the hope that his girl will remain faithful to him while he is away – especially at this critical time of year. A hint of melancholy yet remains.

The original rhymes a, b, a, b, a, b, a, b, which I cannot fluently reproduce in English. Verse renderings by Symonds and Whicher, who are also forced to rhyme a, b, a, b, c, d, c, d (but who both fail to alternate between masculine and feminine rhymes, making all unnecessarily masculine). Discussed and annotated by Walsh. Set by Orff.

CB 138   *Veris leta facies*

Anonymous; known only from CB; followed by German-language piece (CB 138a, *In liehter varwe stat der walt*).

Schumann questions whether stanza 4 is not an accretion, and points to other peculiarities suggestive of corruption – e.g. that the last four lines of stanza 1 and the first four lines of stanza 2 form a thematic unity. Stanza 3 reminds us of the social status claimed by scholars and clerics of the time, not to mention the high esteem in which they evidently held themselves (cf. the topic of knight v. cleric in CB 92, etc., and perhaps the last lines of CB 216).

Set by Orff, omitting stanza 3.

CB 143   *Ecce gratum et optatum*

Anonymous; known only from CB; followed by German stanza (CB 143a: *Ze niwen vroden stat min mut . . .*).

A song of spring and love, of universal rather than personal applicability. In stanza 2, the image is either of spring sucking at summer's breast (*ver estatis ubera* in the manuscript) or, as amended by Schumann, of earth at spring's (*veris tellus ubera*). In stanza 3, the last lines invite us to emulate Paris in happiness (*pares esse Paridis*). He it was who awarded Aphrodite the golden apple for beauty and was in turn rewarded by the winning of Helen. Unfortunately, the conjunction of 'Paris' and 'spring' would evoke irrelevant images in English and I have preferred to work round it.

I follow the rhyme scheme and metre exactly. Verse rendering also by Symonds, who does not. Set by Orff.

CB 145a *Vvere diu werlt alle min*

This verse is described by Olive Sayce as 'enigmatic, as its final lines appear to be incomplete or corrupt'. It is known only from CB, where the penultimate line originally read *daz chunich von Engellant* . . . – that is, 'I would renounce it all if the king of England would but lie in my arms.' A later hand has crossed out *chunich* and substituted *diu chuenegin*, 'the queen', changing the sex of the singer (presumably) from woman to man. Who, in either case, is the object of desire? If a king, Richard the Lionheart is the most generally favoured candidate: if a queen, Eleanor of Aquitaine is the obvious and preferred choice. Part of the enigma lies in its continuing appeal. More than one popular historian ignores the fact that before correction the song spoke of 'the king', asserting that it enjoyed widespread popularity as a medieval jingle and taking Eleanor for granted as its dedicatee.

The archaic verse form has led to the suggestion that it comes from a now lost epic poem (*Oswald*). Its position in CB suggests that it may have been popular in its original 'king' version as a dance song. Perhaps the correction by a later hand does indeed betoken a popular shift of allegiance to the Lionheart's mother.

Set by Orff.

CB 148 *Floret tellus floribus*

Another anonymous spring-and-dance song, known only from CB; followed by a German-language dance refrain (CB 148a, *Nu sin stolz vnde hovisch*). Emendations by Schumann; Latin also in Raby.

CB 149   *Floret silva nobilis*

Anonymous; known only from CB; Latin (*Floret silva . . .*) and German (*Gruonet der walt allenthalben*).

'The woman's complaint of an absent or faithless lover,' writes Olive Sayce (*The Medieval German Lyric 1150–1300*, p. 239), 'is a type very characteristic of the early German lyric.' Sayce points out that this is one of the few instances in which the Latin is clearly modelled on the German, rather than vice versa, partly on formal grounds, partly because the Latin rhymes are unusually imperfect, and partly because the theme is 'not elsewhere attested in the medieval Latin lyric' though common in the German. (Desertion, however, is a significant element in CB 126.)

Set by Orff.

CB 157   *Lucis orto sidere*

Known only from CB, this song – one of several pastourelles – depicts an encounter between a country lass and a comparatively urbane, if predatory, male, from whose viewpoint the outcome is not always successful. (See also CB 158, CB 90.) Schumann observes that one or more stanzas must be missing between stanzas 2 and 3, and another after stanza 7, which forms too abrupt a conclusion.

Superficial reading of the original suggests a typically light-hearted specimen of the genre. But the opening line *[Iam] lucis orto sidere* – 'Now the Morning Star has risen' – would have been immediately recognized by the audience as the start of several hymns including one traditionally sung at Prime. The subsequent Christian imagery of sheep, wolves and pastoral rod soon becomes obtrusive, and this, in the words of Professor Walsh, 'superimposes a further dimension of sophistication. There is a deliberately sustained biblical and liturgical evocation here which contrives to depict the shepherdess as an earthly Virgin Mary. It was a frequent custom for knights of chivalry to dedicate themselves to the Virgin and to carry her portrait on their armour' (*Thirty Poems from the Carmina Burana*).

We are therefore confronted with much the same situation as that of CB 77, *Si linguis angelicis*. Should *Lucis orto* therefore be taken seriously, like an *Ovid moralisé*, or may we regard the biblical and liturgical references as humorously parodical? My choice is apparent and has led me to recast from trochaic to iambic metre for the sake of fluency.

Discussed and annotated by Walsh; Latin also in Raby.

CB 158   *Vere dulci mediante*

An anonymous and perhaps more typical pastourelle than the foregoing; known only from CB. 'Big brother Martin' – a name to conjure with – reminds us that a medieval maiden's honour was a matter of greater family concern than in modern western society. (Note also the brotherly reference in CB 70.) The character is often encountered in medieval literature as a rough and ready, though honest, country type, named after the St Martin referred to in CB 129. Though following the original stanzaic form and rhyme scheme I have again recast from trochaic to iambic measure, whose lighter touch (in English) seems demanded by the nature of the pastourelle.

Verse renderings by Symonds (stanza 1 only) and Whicher (whose girl's final speech is written in the American equivalent of 'Oi be up from Zummerzet' dialect). Latin also in Raby.

CB 167a, 174, 174a   *Three Dance Songs*

These are known only from CB. Rustic festivities marking the advent of spring included the *chorus virginum* – the dancing ring of marriageable girls from whom equally eligible bachelors would choose their (dancing) partners for the coming year.

Swaz hie gat umbe may be interpreted as a teasing song with the sentiment 'Are you men really going to let these women go the whole year without a partner?' (See Dronke, *The Medieval Lyric*, p. 189.)

Veni, veni, venias, with its nonsensical refrain and string of laudatory platitudes, may be interpreted as a response to the foregoing, or at least as universal rather than personal.

Chume, chume . . . is at first sight the German equivalent of its predecessor, though the emotion appears more heartfelt. 'Come and cure me of my pain' is a cry frequently encountered in CB.

Verse rendering of CB 174 by Symonds, under the title 'A Bird's Song of Love'. All three set by Orff.

CB 177   *Stetit puella*

A curious song, also known only from CB, with lines of irregular length and assonance rather than rhyme. Editors previous to Schumann printed the poem as four stanzas, three in Latin and the last in German. The manuscript has three, of which the last is in Latin and German as follows:

> *Stetit puella   bi einem bovme,*
> *scripsit amorem   an eine lovbe.*
>   *dar chom Uenus also fram;*
>   *caritatem magnam,*
>   *hohe minne*
>   *bot si ir manne.*

Verse rendering by Whicher; Latin also in Raby; set by Orff. All of first two stanzas only.

CB 178   *Volo virum vivere*

Anonymous; known only from CB complete, but first four stanzas (in prose) from one another manuscript.

A song in the courtly love tradition, reminiscent of the troubadours in subtlety of theme and elaboration of form. Through four stanzas the poet reviles and renounces the conventional and highly formalized procedures by which a gentleman is to pay court to a lady (as detailed in Andreas Capellanus, *c.* 1185) in favour of a sincere, give-and-take approach, or 'deeply meaningful relationship' as it might now be called. In the fifth he changes his tune and apologizes for his presumption, begging forgiveness and the imposition of a penance. But not without a touch of humour to salve his self-respect. It is not just that he requests punishment (*correptio* is the technical term) to be exacted in her bedroom: the main point is that her granting of *correptio* (anywhere) would, by the rules of the game, mean that she accepted him as her suitor, and he would thus have achieved his object by virtue of the procedures which he first rejected and then 'submitted' himself to.

I follow the rhyme and metre of the original closely, though not everywhere perfectly. Verse rendering also by Waddell in her usual free style. Discussed and annotated by Walsh, who gives more details of the technicalities of courtly love procedure. Translation in O'Donoghue, *The Courtly Love Tradition*. See also Walsh, *Courtly Love in the Carmina Burana*, and a translation of Capellanus by John Parry under the title *The Art of Courtly Love*.

CB 179 *Tempus est iocundum*

Known only from CB; followed by companion piece in German.

The jubilant freedom of this dance song seems to escape the attention of Schumann, who worries over the strophes which are *nicht korrekt gebaut* and rhyme imperfectly, if at all. Certain lines, as he says, are clearly defective. An improved reading and eminently sensible interpretation are offered by Dronke (in *The Medieval Lyric*), who presents it, much as Orff sets it, in parts to be sung by various specified soloists and vocal combinations, and with a refrain for everyone to join in.

Verse renderings also by Symonds, who represents it as a male solo entitled 'The Lover and the Nightingale'; Whicher, also as a solo; and Waddell, rather non-committally. Set by Orff, with (understandably) greater insight into its choric potential.

CB 180 *O mi dilectissima*

Known only from CB; followed by German companion piece.

The singer praises the charms of his beloved and recounts how he felt when he first saw her, how ardently he yearns for her now, and what he has in mind as the next stage in the proceedings, which will come as no surprise to the audience. He partly addresses her directly (in stanzas 1, 3, 5, 6) and partly refers to her in the third person (in stanzas 2, 4, 7), with possible repercussions on the intended mode of performance.

More problematical is the refrain: *Mandaliet! mandaliet! / min geselle chomet niet!* The first line, if not exactly nonsense, amounts to a lyrical interjection. For the second, two diametrically opposed interpretations have been proposed. It may mean 'my companion does not complain', i.e. she reciprocates (or at least is compliant), or 'my companion does not come [to me]'. Schumann, following Vogt, favours the former; the latter is argued by Sayce (*The Medieval German Lyric 1150–1300*, p. 241) and favoured by Dronke (*Medieval Latin and the Rise of European Love-Lyric*, p. 303, footnote).

In choosing between interpretations one might enquire whether the tone of the whole is gloomy and pessimistic, or, if not exactly joyful, at least hopeful. Unfortunately, the whole does not seem entirely consistent in this regard; furthermore, as Sayce demonstrates, the refrain does not properly belong to the Latin lyric but seems to have been transferred to it, by the scribe, from 180a.

Orff sets the last three strophes in gloomy mood (*Circum mea pectora . . .*), which indeed they are when so taken out of context, but evidently favours the jollier interpretation of the refrain – a combination which works in the performance if not in the reading.

CB 183   *Si puer cum puellula*

An anonymous song of self-evident import, known only from CB. It is probably the start of something longer, perhaps with a story-line. Corrupt text; emendations by Schumann. Verse rendering by Symonds. Set by Orff.

CB 185   *Ich was ein chint*

Known only from CB, this tale of seduction is a quasi-pastourelle sung from the woman's viewpoint in alternate German and Latin lines. What appears as the fourth strophe should probably follow the sixth.

Preferring to render entirely in English, and rather freely at that, I have merely hinted at its macaronic nature by printing the originally Latin lines in italics.

CB 186   *Suscipe, Flos, florem*

Though often printed as one, this poem in leonine hexameter (known only from CB) is clearly in two parts. The first is a rather precious affirmation of praise and fidelity in which the poet both addresses his beloved as a rose (cf. CB 77) and offers her the rose which is symbolic of his love (an equally common medieval image). The second amounts to a proverb.

Verse renderings by Symonds, Waddell.

CB191   *Estuans intrinsecus*
('The Archpoet's Confession')

The Archpoet is known in all important respects save by name, date and biographical detail: see Introduction, p. 45. His *Confession* – a title accorded it in the thirteenth century – is known from no fewer than thirty-two manuscripts (seven in England), and extracts from or variations on parts of it from several others.

It is addressed to his patron, Rainald of Dassel, Archbishop of Cologne, and formally fulfils all the requirements of a true confession, including the request for penance. But it is obvious that the poet's chief literary interest lies in his description of the pleasures of which he nominally repents, and in the arguments by which he considers them, in the long run, to be mitigated.

The poem – for this, in fact, is how we read it – falls naturally into three distinct sections: the penitent's state of mind, the pleasures of the tavern, and the conclusion.

In stanzas 1 to 3 we are introduced to the inner turmoil to which the poet has been brought by an insight into the haphazardness of his outer life and behaviour. (*Interius* in this manuscript appears as *intrinsecus* in most, but the difference is not critical.) 'Building upon a rock' is an obvious biblical reference, but subsequent images will be drawn as freely from classical as from Christian sources.

In stanzas 4 to 9 he confesses to venery, both actual and unrealized: reference to girls he 'can't possess, except in imagination' may bring to mind Matthew 5, 28. Youth, however, is one mitigating circumstance; another, all the more effective in combination with it, is the character of the city of Pavia in which, presumably, the poem is being written – Rainald is known to have been there on separate occasions in 1162 and 1163. Pavia, in Lombardy, was a university town attracting students from all over Europe specializing in law – a promising clientele for women prepared to take advantage of it.

Stanza 10 deals with his penchant for gambling. He may have lost the shirt off his back, but toiling at his vocation ('verse-begetting') renders the inner man warm as a smithy.

Stanzas 11 to 13 mark the pleasures of the tavern as third upon the charge-sheet. The opening of stanza 12

> *Meum est propositum*
> *in taberna mori,*
> *ut sint vina proxima*
> *morientis ori . . .*

became perhaps better known than *Estuans intrinsecus ira vehementi*, being frequently quoted in other manuscripts and forming the basis of at least one derivative drinking song. The stanza concludes with an untranslatable pun:

> *. . . tunc cantabunt letius*
> *angelorum chori:*
> *'Sit Deus propitius*
> *huic potatori'.*

Luke 18, 13, has 'God be merciful to me, a sinner' – '*huic peccatori*', as opposed to *potatori*, 'drinker'. Under all this biblical impressiveness one may lose sight of the humour implicit in the poet's taste in wine. As we shall be reminded by the sardonic reference to 'gentle wine, mellifluous in flavour' of CB 197, tavern wine was probably somewhat ropier than today's own-brand plonk, and certainly inferior to the contents of Rainald's cellar. But the latter is rejected as being surreptitiously 'watered down' by the Archbishop's butler (no doubt as a disguise for theft rather than out of a prelate's stinginess), and only the tavern's juice has the guts needed by the poet to keep his inspiration active.

Stanzas 14 to 19 develop this theme, but are taken from – indeed, constitute – an earlier poem by the same author. The gist is clear: our hero is no adherent of the 'ivory tower' school of poetry but craves food, drink and noisy conviviality to sustain his gregarious muse. This passage is clearly an interpolation; but to excise it on grounds of critical integrity, as urged by some purists, seems just the sort of gesture required to provoke the Archpoet to the medieval equivalent of a two-fingered response.

Stanzas 20 to 25 conclude the Confession in superficially conventional terms, though not without side-swipes at unidentified members of the Archbishop's retinue who, while not guiltless themselves, appear to have been spreading tales about the poet's behaviour. It would be nice to think that the Archpoet was aware that under Judaic law 'the first stones' were to be cast by the principal witnesses.

One can well imagine a real-life situation in which the Archpoet is made aware of rumours, or a specific piece of slander, which Rainald shows signs of being adversely affected by, and producing a 'confession' calculated to appease his patron by appealing to his sense of humour.

The whole is written in goliardic verse rhyming a, a, a, a, faultlessly and in strict measure throughout. I have taken some liberties in both respects, and, as usual, have found it necessary to recast each stanza's four long lines as eight short ones. It is a fact of life that English takes up more space than its Latin equivalent.

There is a verse rendering by Symonds, who succeeds in sustaining four rhymes per stanza, though with such occasional infelicities as 'All that Venus bids me do / do I with erection'. Whicher, in a mighty *tour de force*, goes so far as to double the rhymes (a, b, a, b, a, b, a, b, a, b) and, for good measure, throws in the additional five stanzas which constitute CB 191a in the manuscript (*Cum sit fama multiplex / de te divulgata*) but are not now thought to be of the same authorship. Waddell essays seventeen stanzas with her customary distaste for strict metre. Discussed and annotated by Walsh; Latin also in Raby, omitting stanzas 14 to 19. First five stanzas set by Orff (*Estuans interius*).

CB 193   *Denudata veritate*

The dispute between Wine and Water, composed by an unidentified 'Peter' referred to in the final stanza, is known from five manuscripts. That of Benediktbeuern breaks off at stanza 12, line 3. One of the sources from which the remainder is compiled is a manuscript in the Bodleian Library, which is described by Bischoff – with apparently unconscious irony – as 'partly damaged by water'.

Argument between two disputants was a form much favoured in the Middle Ages. We have already encountered that between the respective adherents of knights and clerics in the story of Phyllis and Flora (CB 92), while in the same section as that under consideration is another devoted to the rivalry of wine and water. Amongst other recorded 'Disputes' of the time are those between Wine and Beer, Summer and Winter, and Ganymede and Helen (Helen wins).

The poet's real starting-point is a revulsion against the habit of drinking diluted wine. For literary effect, this is translated into the more even-handed proposition that wine and water, while equally honourable in themselves, should not be mixed together. It is then taken a stage further and represented as debate between personifications of the disputants. A flavour of the original which cannot adequately be conveyed in translation is the fact that *aqua* is feminine while *vinum*, though grammatically neuter, inevitably comes across as masculine. Corresponding he/she personifications do not come off well in English and I refrain from any such attempt.

For the second half of stanza 27, Bischoff (editor of this section of the critical edition) favours:

> *Multi ferre te viderunt*
> *sordes, que non perierunt*
> *per diei spatium!*

which may be rendered:

> We've all seen you in the throes of
> filth and much you can't dispose of
> in the course of a whole day!

My rendering follows the Bodleian manuscript and another from Paris reading *Multi sepe te biberunt / qui per sordes perierunt / per diei spatium!* which surely gives more point to wine's triumph, and, as Symonds says, 'shows that people in the Middle Ages were fully alive to the perils of contaminated wells'. (In fact, Europe was considerably more hygienic in the twelfth century than in the sixteenth and seventeenth.)

The second half of stanza 15 reminds us that there were dull dons and lively lecturers then as now – but as teachers were mostly self-employed in those enlightened days, and consequently earned according to their popularity, it was to their advantage to attract students rather than drive them away.

I follow the metrical and rhyme scheme closely throughout. Verse renderings also by Symonds and Whicher.

CB 196   *In taberna quando sumus*

The greatest drinking song of the Middle Ages, if not ever, is known in its entirety only from CB and owes its effectiveness to a combination of verbal effervescence and tightly controlled structure. Two verses set the scene, describe the inmates and detail the gambling activities. Two enumerate characters of the medieval world to whom rounds of wine are drunk. Two more list the characters who do the drinking. The last asserts the drinkers' defiance of what the rest of the world may say – presumably the teetotal part, since there cannot be much of it left in terms of profession or occupation.

There are satisfying links and contrasts between stanzas and sections. Stanza 1 leads into stanza 2 by the promise of further information. Stanza 3, on the appropriate word *primo*, starts a new section which stanza 4 continues without break, itself leading into the next section with the introductory line *bibunt omnes sine lege*. Stanzas 5 and 6 also constitute an integral section, listing drinkers individually but reaching the all-embracing climax in *bibunt centum, bibunt mille*. Even this line is both conclusion and introduction in one: it clearly rounds off the enumeration of drinkers, yet the final verse promptly takes up the numerical theme by relating it to the amount of money involved. By thus harking back to an opening theme (*ubi nummus est pincerna*, 'where control over your drinking is exerted only by the amount of ready cash you can put up for it'), it prepares us for a rousing finish in what might be described as the key of the tonic. Quite apart from its merits as a drinking song, *In taberna* must be accounted, in structural terms, one of the most accomplished pieces of the Buranian manuscript.

As so often in the collection, the content is more subtle than may appear at first sight. The lists of toasters and toastees parody parts of the Roman liturgy: amongst *Orationes Diversae* appended to the *Missae Votivae* are to be found Masses *pro navigantibus, pro publice poenitantibus*, even *pro peregrinantibus et iter agentibus* (see Walsh, *Thirty Poems from the Carmina Burana*). The drunk-to parallel the prayed-for.

Raby, in *Secular Latin Poetry*, quotes an irresistible parallel which begins with the same hymn-opener as CB 157:

> *Iam lucis orto sidere*
> *statim oportet bibere:*
> *bibamus nunc egregire*
> *et rebibamus hodie.*
>
> *Quicumque vult esse frater*
> *bibat semel, bis, ter, quater:*
> *bibat semel et secundo,*
> *donec nihil sit in fundo.*
>
> *Bibat ille, bibat illa,*
> *bibat servus et ancilla,*
> *bibat hera, bibat herus:*
> *ad bibendum nemo serus.*
>
> *Potatoribus pro cunctis,*
> *pro captivis et defunctis,*
> *pro imperatore et papa,*
> *bibo vinum sine aqua . . .* [etc.]

Toasts six to nine are respectively made to *sororibus vanis, militibus silvanis, fratribus perversis* and *monachis dispersis*. The 'sisters' are nuns

and described as 'worldly', 'worthless' or perhaps 'fruitless'. The 'wood-
land military' may be huntsmen (Walsh) or, at a period when profession-
al fighters were out of a job in times of peace, bands of unemployed
soldiers who wandered the countryside making a nuisance of themselves
between wars. Friars who lose their sense of vocation become, in the
etymological sense of the word, 'perverts' as opposed to 'converts'.
Monks, similarly, may be said to 'disperse' if they give up their essentially
cloistered way of life. All four categories, then, are in some sense
renegades or drop-outs – ideal candidates for the unholy orders described
in CB219.

I follow the metre and rhyme scheme closely. To allow the incorpora-
tion of desired elements where they do not fit strict metre, the original is
'tumbling verse', or what G. M. Hopkins would describe as 'sprung
rhythm'. Naturally, I have of similar necessity 'sprung' mine in different
places. I make no apology for 'tinker, tailor, soldier, sailor': as a
traditional stocklist of characters it serves the same ultimate purpose as
the original. (The Latin list has been said to parody parts of *Laude Sion*, a
hymn of St Thomas Aquinas on the Eucharist. But as this was written in
1262 we must draw other conclusions, only one of which is that St
Thomas Aquinas was in fact parodying *In taberna*.)

Verse rendering by Symonds (just the opening) and Whicher (com-
plete). Discussed and annotated by Walsh. Set by Orff.

CB197 *Dum domus lapidea*

Dum domus is a bibulous parody (or travesty, as Bischoff prefers) of
CB62, *Dum Diane vitrea*, q.v. It is, unfortunately, too corrupt and
incomplete to cast much light on the interpretational problems of its
model, and is not recorded in any other known manuscript. Stanza 1, 3, *et
a fratris rosea*, is a rather pointless reproduction of the original line, and
stanza 3, line 3, is missing, as are the first two lines of stanza 5. After
stanza 4, there are few positive resemblances to the original. The manu-
script puts stanza 6 before stanza 5, but Bischoff reverses this order,
following Schumann (and the model).

The references to wine 'sweet as nectar' are surely ironic: one thinks
immediately of the Archpoet and his perverse tastes (CB 191).

I follow the metric and rhyming scheme of the Latin closely, but in
places have paralleled the effect rather than the words by more closely

parodying my own English version of CB 62. The result may be described as a dog-Latin's dinner.

Dum domus is studiously ignored in most commentaries. Helen Waddell (*W.S.*, p. 164), makes a promising start: *When the pub is sighted / in the market square / every face is lighted / with its rosy flare, / then says every cheery soul, / 'Could you find a better hole?'* But she soon comes to an end. This is a pity, as it is one of her best translations.

CB 207   *Tessera, blandita*

Parts I and II are known only from CB. The whole is written in hexameters with various rhyming effects: Part I has none, II has end-rhyme, III is leonine, IV is alternately leonine and triple-rhymed. My lapse into limerick for the last verses, though in each case a foot longer than the original, may be explained by setting out the Latin in the following format:

> Hi tres ecce canes
> segnes, celeres et inanes
> sunt mea spes,
> quia dant michi res
> et multiplicant es . . .

CB 210   *Qui cupit egregium*

This anonymous mini-treatise on how to play chess is written in leonine distychs (rhyming at half-lines, which I have separated in translation), and is recorded in no fewer than fifteen other manuscripts. As an instruction manual it leaves something to be desired.

CB 216   *Tempus hoc letitie*

'I have recently learned that you live dissolutely, preferring play to work, and strumming your guitar while others are at their studies,' writes a medieval father to his student son (quoted in C. Warren Hollister,

Medieval Europe). The dissolute life-style of university students also features in CB 6, *Florebat olim studium*, where it is castigated, and CB 75, *Omittamus studia*, where it is enjoined. Here, at least, there is some excuse for it – a holiday, or rag day perhaps, in which the strumming of guitars and yet jollier indulgences are positively *de rigueur*. Even Ovid, the favourite classical author of the period, can be left to kick his heels in the draughty corridors and echoing halls of a temporarily abandoned *alma mater*. 'Who cares what the world may say?' – perhaps here is a reference to the killjoy townies who will go grubbing and grumbling about in their drab, grey, uneducated lives while the 'young at heart' let their hair down and 'join the celebrations'.

Verse rendering also by Whicher.

CB 219   *Cum 'In orbem universum'*

Anonymous, but ending on a verse adapted from Walter of Châtillon. Known from nine manuscripts, of which CB contains the longest version (though not itself complete).

'Go ye into all the world, and preach the gospel to every creature' (Mark 16, 15) are the words whose Latin embodiment forms the starting point of this ingeniously sustained satire. At a period of history when new monastic orders were being founded – Cluniac in 909, Carthusian in 1084, Cistercian in 1098, Dominicans and Franciscans by the time CB was being compiled – this announcement of the establishment and rules of the *Ordo vagorum*, 'Order of Tramps and Vagrants', would have been particularly appreciated. One might see it as the medieval equivalent of a spoof manifesto introducing a new political party.

Like all new orders, it declares itself open to (in effect) 'all right-minded people', i.e. those already in sympathy with its aims, and outlines the rules of the Order as relating to liturgy (no matins, which the Benedictines observed at two a.m.: who in his right mind wants to get up so early?), clothing (bare minimum) and behaviour (be of good cheer and avoid physical discomfort).

The piece abounds in easily overlooked biblical references. My chapter-and-verse reference to St John is gratuitous; attention may also be drawn to Matthew 10, 9–10, 'Provide neither gold, nor silver, nor brass in your purses, nor scrip for your journey, neither two coats, neither shoes, nor yet staves: for the workman is worthy of his meat.'

I follow the goliardic measure with slight metrical latitude, the order of verses recommended by Bischoff, and a generally accepted completion of stanza 6 (which in *Buranus* ends at line 2).

Verse renderings also by Symonds and Whicher. Richly discussed and annotated by Walsh.

CB222   *Ego sum abbas*

An obvious satellite of CB219 (above), known only from CB. Cockaigne is an imaginary land of luxury and idleness: see *Brewer's Dictionary of Phrase and Fable*. The final exclamation, *Wafna!* is cognate with 'weapons' (cf. modern German *Waffen*) and so equivalent to *aux armes!* as a cry for help.

Rendering also by Symonds. Set by Orff.

CB2*   *Ich lob die liben frowen min*

This German love lyric is a late addition to the CB text and not recorded elsewhere, though line 6 is borrowed from Heinrich von Morungen (died *c.* 1222).

Dronke (*The Medieval Lyric*, p. 137) notes – not in this connection – that the word *frowe, frouwe* had become 'fashionable' in Morungen's time in place of the comparatively unassuming *wip* (cognate with *wife*), and quotes a poem by the contemporary Walther von der Vogelweide in which the two terms are compared: ' "Woman" [*wip*],' says Walther, 'will always be woman's highest name – it honours her more than "lady" [*frouwe*].' Ironically, *Weib* has come to bear unflattering connotations in modern German.

CB16*   *Chramer, gip die varwe mier*

These verses, which I include chiefly because they are set by Orff and will therefore be known to many readers, are sung by Mary Magdalene in a passion play constituting part of the *Fragmenta Burana* and numbered 16 in the CB supplement.

The play is written in a mixture of Latin and German. It opens with the portrayal of incidents from the earthly life of Jesus, with parts for Herod, Pilate and the Pharisees. There follows a scene involving Mary Magdalene, a chorus of *puellae* and a chapman (*mercator; chramer*). Three times she sings songs in Latin and German asserting the pleasures of life and the pride she takes in the pursuit of her profession: three times an angel appears and draws her attention to the grace of God which is made available through Jesus. She finally accepts, singing:

> *Hinc, ornatus seculi,*   *vestium candores!*
> *procul a me fugite,*   *turpes amatores!*
> *ut quid nasci volui,*   *que sum defedanda*
> *et ex omni genere*   *criminum notanda!*

The love described in these verses belongs to the courtly tradition, no doubt with ironic intent. *Hoech gemuet* is a courtly key-word for that nobility of soul which true love is supposed to inspire, and the image of binding oneself as a vassal is used for the fealty or fidelity accorded to his lady by the properly behaved lover.

CB3* *Iam dudum estivalia*

This beautiful winter poem, known from three manuscripts, was modelled by Der Marner on a German original by Walther von der Vogelweide. It is a late addition to the CB text. The lines of stanza 1 all rhyme on -*a*, those of 2 on -*e*, 3 on -*i*, 4 on -*o* and 5 on -*u*. I follow rhyme and metre exactly.

Appendix C
Glossary of Names

The purpose of these notes is to explain the significance of classical, biblical and literary personages encountered in the text, not to offer complete biographies. Note that in medieval orthography *-ae* is simplified to *-e*, so that (for example) the classical 'Actaeon' appears as 'Acteon'.

ACTEON (ACTAEON)   Acteon, Lampos, Erythreus and Philogeus are the four horses who successively draw Apollo's chariot across the sky and thus 'rule' different times of day – as explained in CB 66.

ADONIS   A beautiful youth from Cyprus, loved by Aphrodite/Venus, accidentally killed while hunting boar (according to Ovid). Venus's sorrow is referred to in 'Phyllis and Flora', CB 92.

AENEAS   A son of Aphrodite; Trojan hero of Virgil's *Aeneid*; lover of Dido. Their tragic love-story forms the subject of three *carmina Burana* (CB 98–100), and other references are frequent, e.g. CB 3.

ALCIBIADES   Flora's clerical hero in 'Phyllis and Flora' (CB 92). The name itself is heroic, being that of a pupil of Socrates who later became a famous Athenian politician and general (*c.* 450–404 BC). It may carry the suggestion that he is no less 'manly' for not being a knight.

AMALRICH = AMALRIC I   Born in 1135, died 1174. King of the crusaders' state of Jerusalem, 1163–74. Son of Fulk of Anjou and Melisande of Jerusalem. Conquered Fatimid Egypt in 1168 with help of Byzantine Emperor Manuel Comnenus, as commemorated in CB 51a.

AMBROSE, SAINT   Born 339, died 397. Bishop of Milan, under whom Theodosius established Christianity as the official religion of the Empire. Wrote on ethics and ascetics: his *De officiis ministrorum* dealt particularly with the ethics of priests. Renowned hymn-writer.

AMOR   An alias of Cupid, q.v., hence the god or personification of erotic love. More frequently referred to in medieval than in classical literature. Prominent in CB 87, CB 92.

APHRODITE (= CYTHEREA, DIONE, VENUS)   Originally the Greek goddess of sex. Identified by the Romans as Venus, and under this name shifted towards the romantic end of the affective spectrum. Referred to as Cytherea in the original Latin in 'Phyllis and Flora', after the island of Cythera (off Laconia) where she was held to have risen from the waves and where a famous shrine was dedicated to her; also, again in the Latin, as Dione, the consort of Zeus before his association with Hera, who appears as a synonym for her daughter Venus in CB 72.

APOLLO   Greek god of music and song, hence the source of poetic talent or inspiration. Also called Phoebus, 'shining', and under this name later confused with the sun-god Helios. Both attributes are implicit in 'the Archpoet's Confession', CB 191. As sun-god, also implicit in CB 62 as the 'brother' of Diana's 'crystal lantern' (the moon) and as he whose chariot is drawn across the sky by Acteon and others in CB 66.

APRIL   In CB 136, personification of the month April, hence of spring: from *aperire*, 'to open', as being the time of year when earth unfolds and nature opens up.

ARGUS   The hundred-eyed giant referred to in CB 70. Son of Zeus by Niobe, he was set by Hera to watch over the heifer into which Io had been metamorphosed. At Zeus's instigation, Hermes (Mercury) lulled him to sleep with a flute and then cut off his head. His eyes were subsequently transplanted by Hera into peacocks' tails.

AUGUSTINE, SAINT   Aurelius Augustinus, born AD 354, died 430. Bishop of Hippo, author of *De civitate Dei*. His combination of Christian theology with elements of Platonic philosophy exercised a profound influence on medieval religious and political thought. (CB 6.)

AURORA   Roman goddess of dawn, often represented as driving her chariot across the sky. Referred to in 'Phyllis and Flora', CB 92.

BACCHUS   ('riotous') A name of Dionysus, the effeminate god of wine (popular rather than Olympian). This name, which was also used by the Greeks, was the only one the Romans used. Intoxication is often associated with inspiration in classical literature, and the association is carried over in 'the Archpoet's Confession'. See also MARTIN, SILENUS.

BENEDICT, SAINT   Born *c.* 480, died *c.* 550. Educated at Rome, which he fled in disgust to become a hermit. Developed monastic principles subsequently embodied as the Rule of St Benedict, and is thus regarded as the founder of western monasticism. (CB 6.)

BLANCHEFLEUR (also BLANCHEFLOR, BLANZIFLOR)   Heroine of the romance *Floire et Blancheflor* (*c.* 1170). Daughter of a Provençal noblewoman held captive by a Spanish king, the father of Floire. On discovery of their love, the king sells her into slavery. Floire traces her to Babylon, rescues her and eventually returns to make her his queen. (CB77.)

BUCEPHALUS ('bull-headed')   Alexander the Great's favourite horse. Used metaphorically rather than literally in 'Phyllis and Flora'.

CATO   Marcus Porcius Cato, 95–46 BC (also grandfather of same name and similar character, 234–149 BC). Stoical writer and politician, renowned for his stern uprightness and moral rectitude – thus adding humour to the reference in *Florebat olim studium* (CB6).

CODRUS   The personification of poverty, after the 'begging poet' at whom Juvenal pokes fun in *Satires*, III, 203:

> *What did friend Codrus own? One truckle bed, too short for even a midget nympho; one marble-topped sideboard on which stood six little mugs; beneath it, a pitcher and an up-ended bust of Chiron . . .*

(from the translation by Peter Green, *Juvenal: the Sixteen Satires*, Penguin Classics, 1967). Juvenal's popularity amongst twelfth-century literati explains the frequency of reference to his characters. (CB1, CB19.)

COMNENUS   See MANUEL.

CORONIS   Associated, like Niobe, with tears, as in CB72. A Thessalian princess, daughter of Phlegyas and posthumous mother of Asclepius (Coronides) by Apollo. Apollo had her killed for her infidelity, the unborn Asclepius being snatched from her womb and subsequently reared by Chiron.

CUPID (also called AMOR; and equivalent to Greek EROS)   Roman god of sexual desire (cupidity), later of love in general. Son of Venus, represented as a 'boy-god' or cherub (*deus puerilis*), often blindfold, as he is no respecter of persons and tends to fire his darts or arrows at random – see especially *Amor tenet omnia*, CB87. This may explain why he does not answer for himself when consulted by Phyllis and Flora (CB92) as to the relative merits of knights and clerics – they are probably all the same to him.

CYTHER(E)A   See APHRODITE.

DAVUS, GETA, BYRRIA   Stock figures of menial service in several twelfth-century comedies, named from slaves in Terence. (The originals of 'Tom, Dick and Harry' in CB193.)

DECIUS   The medieval personification of dice and god of dicing, mentioned by name in the original Latin in CB222, CB219, and elsewhere.

DIANA   Roman goddess of light (with a counterpart in Dianus/Janus, the god of light – cf. *dies*, 'day'). As opposed to Janus, particularly associated with the night, hence with moonlight and the moon itself. The moon becomes 'Diana's crystal lamp' in CB62. Equivalent to the Greek goddess Artemis, whose brother, Apollo, is referred to in the following line.

DIDO   Queen and legendary founder of Carthage; lover of Aeneas, q.v., according to Virgil (in defiance of historical possibility). When Aeneas abandoned her in quest of his historic mission to found Rome, she impaled herself on his sword and so became an archetype of the tragic heroine.

DIDYMUS   See THOMAS.

DIONE   See APHRODITE.

EROS   See CUPID.

ERYTHREUS   See ACTEON.

FAUNS   'Similar to Greek satyrs, but gentler,' says Betty Radice (*Who's Who in the Ancient World*). The goat-legged humanoids take their name from Faunus, the Roman equivalent of Pan. Encountered in their gentler form as attendants of Bacchus in the original Latin of 'Phyllis and Flora' (CB92), but regarded as a *genus demoniorum* in CB54.

FLORA   The friend of Phyllis in CB92 would have been named after the Roman goddess of flowers and trees. Hers is one of the most popular female names in medieval literature, occurring nine times in CB alone. She also appears as *consors Phyllidis* in CB59. The goddess, a personification of spring, was celebrated in a flower festival, the *ludi florales*, which the Romans held every April. (See CB138.)

FORTUNA   Classical goddess of fate or fortune, equivalent to Greek Tyche but worshipped more by the Romans and represented by them variously with a rudder (guidance), a ball (unsteadiness), or a horn of plenty (distributor of goods). A very active member of the medieval pantheon, she was almost exclusively depicted as controlling human destinies from the hub of her 'wheel'. She is so illustrated on the first page of CB in its present binding (see cover picture). (CB16, CB17.)

GANYMEDE   A servant or equerry (CB92). Originally a beautiful youth fancied by Zeus and carried off by him to become his cupbearer in place of Hebe. Hence, often, a personification of homosexuality.

GRACES   Originally three daughters of Zeus – Thalia, Euphrosyne, Aglaia: the embodiments of youth, beauty and innocence. Traditionally depicted as a unified group with fingers interlaced, as in Botticelli's *Primavera* and as described in 'Phyllis and Flora' (CB 92).

GREGORY, SAINT   Born 540, died 604. Pope Gregory I ('the Great') from 590. His papacy saw the recognition of the papal state and the division between the Orthodox and Catholic churches. Writings include *The Book of Pastoral Rule*, in effect a guide to the right living of bishops, and works of biblical exegesis following the teaching of Augustine (q.v.). Profoundly influenced liturgy and church music; the originator of Gregorian chant.

HECUBA   As mentioned in CB 16, the natural exemplar of one who has risen high and fallen low. Originally the wife of Priam, she suffered many vicissitudes after the Trojan War and eventually died metamorphosed into a bitch.

HELEN   Even today, Helen remains the most exhaustively yet least conclusively analysed of all classical figures – perhaps because she is careful never to emerge as a person but always as a symbol, to be reinterpreted by each literary generation according to its own lights. She was the daughter of Zeus and Leda, sister of Castor and Pollux, wife of Menelaus. Her abduction by Paris (q.v.) led to the Trojan War. In Greek legend she is variously portrayed as in some sense guilty of causing the war or else as an innocent victim of it and her own beauty. In the twelfth century the more mainstream 'guilty' aspect tended to prevail, possibly under the influence of traditionally anti-feminist aspects of church doctrine, or with the rise of mariolatry as a counterbalance to this ideological defect. However, part of the 'innocent' tradition, first explored by Stesichorus, held that the real Helen remained in Egypt while the figure which went to Troy was only a phantom in her guise. As Dronke points out in connection with CB 77, this tradition would have been known to the twelfth century through Servius.

HESPERUS   The evening star: a personification of the planet now called Venus, which, in its guise as the morning star, was also known as Lucifer or Phosphorus. The 'drawing of dewdrops' by Hesperus in CB 62 reflects the view of plant transpiration as moisture being drawn from or sucked up by the evening star.

HIPPOLYTUS   A male model of chastity popular in medieval literature (CB 178, CB 191). He was the son of Theseus by Hyppolyte, queen of the Amazons. Theseus later married Phaedra. Failing in an attempt to seduce her stepson, Phaedra accused him to Theseus of dishonourable advances. The father thereupon had Hippolytus killed.

JEROME, SAINT   Born *c.* 342, died 420. Educated at Rome. Priest, preacher and biblical scholar who, in the hermit's cell near Bethlehem, where he eventually died, translated the Bible into Latin. The resultant 'Vulgate' became the authoritative Bible of the Middle Ages; from it are drawn all biblical references and many turns of phrase encountered in the *Carmina Burana.* (See CB 6.)

JOVE   See JUPITER.

JULIANA   An uncommon female name, encountered in CB 85.

JUNO (Greek, HERA)   To the Romans, the queen of heaven and goddess of women, especially wives. Wife of Jupiter.

JUPITER, JOVE   To the Romans, the 'god-father' (*Jovis Pater*) and hence the chief deity. Considerably less colourful than his Greek counterpart Zeus, though equally unrenowned for marital fidelity – a fact referred to in CB 3. 'Happy as Jove', in CB 116, is a common medieval comparison.

LAMPOS   See ACTEON.

LEAH   In CB 6, the 'tender-eyed' daughter of Laban, sister of Rachel (q.v.), wife of Jacob, mother of seven sons (Genesis 29, 15 ff.).

LUCRETIA   A model of feminine chastity, probably legendary, Lucretia was the wife of Tarquinius Collatinus. She is portrayed by classical authors as having killed herself for shame after being raped by Sextus, son of Tarquinius Superbus.

MANUEL COMNENUS   Manuel I (1122–80), Emperor of Byzantium from 1143. As recorded in CB 51a, assisted Amalrich in conquest of Egypt. Grandson of Alexius Comnenus, whose request to Urban II for assistance against the Seljuks led to the preaching of the First Crusade.

MARTHA   In CB 6, the archetypal household-runner and domestic hard worker. Sister of Mary. (Luke 10, 38 ff.)

MARTIN   A common European name, after the subsequently canonized fourth-century Bishop of Tours. An incident in the life of St Martin – the donation of his cloak to a poor pilgrim – is mentioned in the begging poem CB 129: the garment in question became an official relic in the eighth century. A patron saint of France, he was also that of innkeepers and reformed drunkards, having been born on Bacchus's day, 11th November. The name suggests bluff, rustic honesty – a nice touch for the 'big brother' of the wench assaulted in CB 158.

MARY (sister of Martha)   The 'Mary' of CB 6 is the one who left her sister Martha to do the work while she sat at Jesus's feet, and heard his word (Luke 10, 39).

MARY (mother of Jesus)   The Holy Virgin is referred to chiefly by title rather than by name, and sometimes so obliquely that it is hard to distinguish between reference and resonance (CB 77, CB 157, etc.). A tendency of medieval poets to describe and even address her in terms of startling physicality became particularly marked in the thirteenth century.

MERCURY   Originally the Roman god of commerce, later identified (tenuously) with the Greek messenger-god Hermes. It was the latter who fluted Argus to sleep: see ARGUS, and CB 70. His 'marriage', represented as part of the saddle-decorations in 'Phyllis and Flora', relates to a fifth-century work by Martianus Capella, still much read in the twelfth century. The bride was Philology.

MINERVA   Roman goddess with a heavy portfolio of responsibility for wisdom, war, arts and trades; even also credited with the invention of musical instruments. This adds point to her dropping of all other activities in order to weave and decorate a caparison for the horse on which Phyllis rides to Cupid's court in CB 92.

MORPHEUS   God of dreams and human visions – the name means 'shaper' or 'fashioner': a son of Hypnos, god of sleep. Well known from Ovid's *Metamorphoses*, one of the most popular classical works of the twelfth century. Both facts render plausible the emendation of the manuscript's 'Orpheus' to 'Morpheus' in CB 62.

NEPTUNE (Greek, POSEIDON)   Best known as god of the sea, but represented in CB 92 as the donor of Phyllis's fantastic mule. Originally a sky-god, often thought of as a horse that shakes the earth with its hooves.

ORPHEUS   In the manuscript of CB 62, is emended by some editors to Morpheus, q.v. Archetypal poet-musician who, with the lyre given him by Apollo (q.v.), could charm anyone and anything – even to the extent of charming his wife Eurydice out of Pluto's underworld.

OVID   Publius Ovidius Naso, Roman poet, born Sulmo (Sulmona) 43 BC, died AD 17–18 at Tomis (Costanza), by the Black Sea, in exile some offence against Augustus Caesar of which the details can only be surmised. Author of humorous, erotic and romantic poetry and the most popular of all classical writers during the twelfth century, especially for his *Metamorphoses*. Frequently mentioned; for example, in CB 193 and CB 216.

PARIS   A son of Priam, Paris is portrayed by Homer as responsible for the Trojan War through his abduction of Helen, wife of Menelaus. In other accounts the abduction fulfilled a reward from Aphrodite, who offered the best of three bribes when Paris was called upon to adjudicate between herself, Hera and Athene in a beauty contest. Medieval references generally emphasize his good fortune at having won the

most beautiful woman in the world (CB 111; see also the note to
CB 143). As the name of Phyllis's beloved knight in CB 92, Paris may
have been selected to suggest romantic qualities, as a balance to
Alcibiades, Flora's cleric, whose name bears military connotations.

PEGASUS   In CB 92, Flora's horse is portrayed as a descendant of
Pegasus, the winged horse which sprang from the blood of Medusa
when Perseus struck off her head. He was later captured by Beller-
ophon. In attempting to fly to heaven, the latter fell to earth; but
Pegasus continued the journey and dwells to this day among the stars.

PETER, SAINT   Keeper of the keys of the gates to Heaven (CB 10).

PHILOGEUS   See ACTEON.

PHILOMEL, PHILOMENA   Popular medieval personification of the
nightingale. From the complex and partly garbled story of Philomela.
Raped by her brother-in-law King Tereus of Thrace, she and her
equally maltreated sister Procne killed the latter's son and served his
flesh up at the father's table. In course of the inevitable pursuit, all three
were turned into birds. According to Ovid (*Metamorphoses*), Philo-
mela became a nightingale. In view of this tragic background, the
nightingale is understandably credited with 'complaining', or at least
singing 'plaintively'. Nightingales are mentioned in CB 62, CB 92,
CB 138, etc., and (not under the name Philomel) in many of the
German songs. Reference to nightingales in medieval Latin often
suggests German provenance or influence.

PHOEBUS   In CB 138, equivalent to Apollo, q.v.

PHYLLIS   She who jeopardizes her honour by loving a knight (CB 92)
bears a pastoral name popular with poets from Virgil onwards. The
original Phyllis was a Thracian princess who committed suicide in the
mistaken belief that her fiancé had forsaken her. Etymologically,
Phyllis = 'foliage'.

RACHEL   In CB 6, Laban's daughter, whom Jacob loved more pas-
sionately than her elder sister Leah (q.v.); he married her (though he
had to marry the elder sister first) but she proved barren (Genesis 29,
15 ff.).

SILENUS   The original *sileni* were satyrs. From them crystallized the
character of Silenus – an old, fat, bald drunkard, who had reared
Bacchus (Dionysus) and now, borne on an ass, accompanies him
everywhere, with others of his tribe dancing attendance. Although
represented as utterly incapable in his brief appearance at the climax of
'Phyllis and Flora' (CB 92), Silenus was classically recognized as not
just intoxicated but also inspired – an association reflected in 'The
Archpoet's Confession'. See also Bacchus.

SIMON   The repersonification of simony (the buying or selling of ecclesiastical posts, goods, services, favours, etc.), who figures prominently in such complaints and satires as CB1 and CB3. Named after Simon the Sorcerer (Simon Magus) (Acts 8).

THEOCLEA   Girl's name; rare. (CB87.)

THISBE   Girl's name; rare, but figuring in CB70, *Estatis florigero* (and, as such, the singer of *In trutina mentis dubia* and *Dulcissime, totam tibi subdo me*). Hardly from the tragedy of Pyramus and Thisbe, unless – since the classical lovers lived in adjoining houses and communicated through a wall – the poet had in mind a real 'girl next door'.

THOMAS DIDYMUS   A disciple of Jesus, the 'Doubting Thomas' of John 20, 24, referred to in CB193. (Didymus = 'twin'.)

VENUS   Personification or goddess of love, very active in the medieval pantheon. Wife of Vulcan, mother of Cupid. Roman equivalent of Aphrodite, q.v.

VULCAN (Greek, HEPHAISTOS)   Roman god of fire and hence of metalworking, usually depicted as a smith and alternatively known as Mulciber, 'the forger'. Husband of Venus, whose hair he used in the making of equipment for Flora's horse in CB92. Vulcan's 'netting', referred to in CB70, is so finely forged as to be invisible. He fashioned it for the purpose of catching his wife in compromising circumstances with Mars.

Appendix D
Bibliography

The Manuscript

The manuscript is housed in the Bayerische Staatsbibliothek in Munich (München), in two parts:

Clm 4660: the original bound volume found at Benediktbeuern in 1803;
Clm 4660a: an additional fragment later discovered amongst other Buranian material housed in the same library (designated *Fragmenta Burana* by their discoverer, the librarian Wilhelm Meyer).

Carmina Burana

Bischoff, Bernhard (ed.), *Carmina Burana* (photographic facsimile of the original manuscript), New York, Institute of Medieval Music, 1967; with a short but useful introduction

Bulst, W., *Carmina Burana: Lateinisch und Deutsch: Lieder der Vaganten*, Heidelberg, Verlag Lambert Schneider, 1961, 1974; a modern revision of Laistner, q.v.

Fischer, Carl, et al., *Carmina Burana*, Zürich u. München, Artemis Verlag, 1974, reprinted Deutscher Taschenbuch Verlag, 1979; the DTV edition is a readily accessible paperback of the complete text based on the critical edition of Hilka–Schumann–Bischoff, with occasional deviations duly noted; original text verso, line-for-line German verse rendering recto; Latin translated by Fischer, Middle High German by Hugo Kuhn, essay and notes by Günter Bernt

Hilka, A., Schumann, O., Bischoff, B., *Carmina Burana*, Heidelberg, Carl Winter Universitätsverlag; Band I, Text: (1) *Die moralisch-satirischen Dichtungen*, ed. Hilka, Schumann, 1930, 2nd edn 1978, (2) *Die Liebeslieder*, ed. Schumann, 1941, 2nd edn 1971, (3) *Die Trink-und Spielerlieder: Die Geistlichen Dramen: Nachträge*, Schumann (dec'd), Bischoff, 1st edn 1970; Band II, Kommentar: (1) *Einleitung (Die Handschrift der C— B—): Die moralisch-satirischen Dichtungen*, ed. Hilka, Schumann, 1930, 2nd end 1961; these constitute the critical edition now taken as authoritative

Laistner, L., *Golias: Studentenlieder des Mittelalters: aus dem lateinischen*, Stuttgart, 1879; a selection with verse renderings in German; see also Bulst

Peiper, R., *Gaudeamus! Carmina vagorum selecta in usum laetitiae*, Leipzig, 1877; a selection

Raby, F. J. E., *The Oxford Book of Medieval Latin Verse*, Oxford University Press, 1959, numerous reprints; Latin text of 14 pieces including *Si linguis angelicis*, *Dum Diane* and extracts from 'Phyllis and Flora'

Schmeller, J. H., *Carmina Burana*, Stuttgart, 1847, reprinted Leipzig, Verlag Hiersemann, 1938; the first modern edition

Walsh, P. G., *Thirty Poems from the Carmina Burana*, Dept. of Classics, University of Reading, 1976, 3rd printing 1983; includes all the major pieces – *Dum Diane*, 'the Archpoet's Confession', 'Phyllis and Flora', the Wine–Water Debate, *In taberna* and 'The Order of Vagrants', but unfortunately not *Si linguis angelicis*; text based on Hilka–Schumann –Bischoff; extensive discussion and annotations; invaluable

Verse Renderings

Symonds, John Addington, *Wine, Women, and Song*, London, Chatto & Windus, 1884; English verse renderings of some 60 pieces, mostly from CB, not all complete; Latin not given; poetic licence much in evidence

Waddell, Helen, *Mediaeval Latin Lyrics*, London, Constable, 1929, 5th edn 1948, numerous reprints; Latin and parallel English verse translations of 28 pieces from older editions of CB, amongst many from other sources; few major items, not all complete; translations poetically faithful, formally very free

Whicher, George F., *The Goliard Poets*, Westport (Connecticut), Greenwood Press, 1949, copyright renewed 1976, reprinted 1979; Latin and parallel American verse translation of 75 pieces, mostly from CB, not all complete; poetic licence sometimes excessive, but – with a few obtrusive exceptions – formally very accurate

Literary Background

Curtius, E. R., translated by Trask, W. R., *European Literature and the Latin Middle Ages*, London, Routledge & Kegan Paul, 1953, paperback edn 1979; notable for study of schools of rhetoric in development of medieval literature, for analysis of medieval themes and for concept of literary topos; few references to C B

Daiches, D. and Thorlby, A. (eds), *The Medieval World*, Volume II of *Literature and Western Civilisation*, London, Aldus Books, 1973; good background, literary, linguistic and historical

Dronke, Peter, *Medieval Latin and the Rise of European Love-Lyric*, Vol. I, *Problems and Interpretations*, Vol. II, *Medieval Latin Love-Poetry*, Oxford University Press, 2nd edn 1968; Vol. I, essential reading, has one chapter on and many references to C B, with text and commentary on several major pieces including *Dum Diane* and *Si linguis angelicis*; Vol. II provides 150 annotated texts, none from C B

Dronke, Peter, *The Medieval Lyric*, London, Hutchinson, 2nd edn 1978; many references to C B, including revised text and commentary on *Tempus est iocundum*

Ford, Boris (ed.), *Medieval Literature: The European Inheritance*, Pt 2 of Vol. I of *The New Pelican Guide to English Literature*, London, Penguin Books, 1983; general interest, with article on the C B passion play from which comes Mary Magdalene's song *Chramer, gip die varwe mier*

Jackson, W. T. H. (ed.), *The Interpretation of Medieval Lyric Poetry*, London, Macmillan, 1980; includes article on *Dum Diane* by Jackson, another on the Archpoet by Dronke

Jackson, W. T. H., *The Literature of the Middle Ages*, Columbia University Press, 1960; general introduction to background, authors, audience and genres; few references to C B, but non-technical and eminently readable

Raby, F. J. E., *Secular Latin Poetry* (2 vols), Oxford University Press, 1934

Robertson, D. W. jun., *Essays in Medieval Culture*, Princeton University Press, N.J., 1980; anthology of lectures and essays over thirty years including boisterously argumentative analyses of 'Two Poems from the C— B—', namely *Dum Diane* and *Si linguis angelicis*

Sayce, Olive, *The Medieval German Lyric 1150–1300*, Oxford University Press, 1982; invaluable both for background and for chapter devoted to C B

Waddell, Helen, *The Wandering Scholars*, London, Constable, 1927, 7th edn 1934, numerous reprints; long on style and enthusiasm, short on texts and specifics, but many valuable references and observations

Courtly Love

'Courtly love' is a literary term invented in the nineteenth century; the extent to which it corresponds to medieval ideals and terminology has long been a subject of contention.

Andreas Capellanus (Andrew the Chaplain) translated by Parry, John J., *De Arte Honeste Amandi (The Art of Courtly Love)*, New York and London, W. W. Norton & Co., 1969 (originally Columbia University Press, 1941); adequate translation of indispensable text *c*. 1185

Boase, Roger, *The Origin and Meaning of Courtly Love*, Manchester University Press, 1977; subtitled 'A critical study of European scholarship', an invaluable analysis of the subject

Kelly, Douglas, *Medieval Imagination*, University of Wisconsin Press, 1978; 'Rhetoric and the Poetry of Courtly Love'; very scholarly

Lewis, C. S., *The Allegory of Love*, Oxford University Press, 1936, numerous reprints; 'a study in medieval tradition', once influential but now regarded as misleading in many respects

O'Donoghue, Bernard, *The Courtly Love Tradition*, Manchester University Press, 1982; succinct introduction, many useful texts with translations and notes; five from CB include *Volo virum vivere* and *O comes amoris*; also extracts from Capellanus

Stevens, John, *Medieval Romance*, London, Hutchinson University Library, 1973; subtitled 'Themes and Approaches', with particular emphasis on twelfth-century vernacular romances

Topsfield, L. T., *The Troubadours and Love*, Cambridge University Press, 1975, paperback 1978; authoritative chapters on individual troubadours, 1100–1300, with many Provençal texts printed, translated and discussed

Valency, Maurice, *In Praise of Love*, New York, Octagon Books, 1975 1st edn 1958); 'An Introduction to the Love-Poetry of the Renaissance'; good background reading free of technical literary terminology

Walsh, P. G., *Courtly Love in the Carmina Burana*, University of Edinburgh, 1971; inaugural lecture

General Background

Artz, Frederick B., *The Mind of the Middle Ages (An Historical Survey, AD 200–1500)*, University of Chicago Press, 3rd edn (revised) 1980 (original text 1953)

Barber, Richard, *The Knight and Chivalry*, London, Sphere Books, 1974 (originally Longman, 1970)

Bishop, Morris, *The Penguin Book of the Middle Ages*, London, Penguin Books, 1971 (originally American Heritage Publishing Co., 1968)

Braudel, Fernand, translated by Miriam Kochan, revised by Siân Reynolds, *The Structures of Everyday Life*, London, Collins, 1981

Brooke, Rosalind and Christopher, *Popular Religion in the Middle Ages (Western Europe, 1100–1300)*, London, Thames & Hudson, 1984

Foss, Michael, *Chivalry*, London, Michael Joseph, 1975

Gimpel, John, *The Medieval Machine (The Industrial Revolution of the Middle Ages)*, London, Gollancz, 1976

Grabois, Aryeh, *The Illustrated Encyclopedia of Medieval Civilisation*, London: Octopus Books, 1980

Heer, Friedrich, *The Medieval World (Europe from 1100 to 1350)*, London, Sphere Books, 1974 (originally Weidenfeld & Nicolson, 1962)

Hollister, C. Warren, *Medieval Europe – a Short History*, New York, Wiley & Sons, 1964, 5th edn 1982

Huizinga, Johan, *The Waning of the Middle Ages*, London, Penguin Books, 1976, numerous reprints (original text 1924)

Keen, Maurice, *The Pelican History of Medieval Europe*, London, Penguin Books, 1969 (originally *A History of Medieval Europe*, Routledge & Kegan Paul, 1968)

Morrall, John, *The Medieval Imprint*, London, Penguin Books, 1967

Morris, Colin, *The Discovery of the Individual, 1050–1200*, New York, Harper Torchbooks, 1972 (originally SPCK)

Pearsall, Derek and Salter, Elizabeth, *Landscapes and Seasons of the Medieval World*, London, Elek Books, 1973

Radice, Betty, *Who's Who in the Ancient World*, London, Penguin Books, 1971

Reese, Gustave, *Music in the Middle Ages*, London, Dent, 1941, numerous reprints

Warner, Marina, *Alone of All her Sex: the Myth and Cult of the Virgin Mary*, London, Weidenfeld & Nicolson, 1976

Young, Charles (ed.), *The Twelfth-Century Renaissance*, New York, Krieger Publishing Co., 1977

Appendix E
Concordance

DP = David Parlett verse rendering
GW = George Whicher: Latin and verse rendering in *The Goliard Poets* (1949)
JS   = John A. Symonds: verse rendering in *Wine, Women and Song* (1884)
HW = Helen Waddell: Latin and verse rendering in *Mediaeval Latin Lyrics*
       (1929–34)
PW = Latin and notes in P. B. Walsh, *Thirty Poems from the Carmina Burana*
       (1976)
OX = Latin in F. Raby, *The Oxford Book of Medieval Latin Verse* (1959–74)
CO = Set by Carl Orff
lower case initials = version incomplete or extract only
numerals = page numbers

PART I

1	*Manus ferens*	DP	GW146	—	—	—	—	—
2	*Responde, qui*	DP	—	—	—	—	—	—
3	*Ecce torpet*	DP	—	—	—	PW53	—	—
6	*Florebat olim*	DP	GW142	—	—	—	—	—
8	*Licet eger*	—	GW132	—	—	PW59	—	—
10	*Ecce sonat*	DP	gw150	—	—	—	—	—
16	*Fortune plango*	DP	—	—	—	PW61	—	CO
17	*O Fortuna*	DP	GW262	—	—	—	—	CO
19	*Fas et nefas*	DP	—	—	hw188	PW60	—	—
20	*Est modus*	DP	—	—	—	—	—	—
21	*Veritatis veritatum*	—	GW158	—	HW196	—	—	—
24	*Iste mundus*	DP	GW154	JS162	—	PW62	—	—
28	*Laudat rite*	DP	—	—	—	—	—	—
30	*Dum iuventus*	DP	GW152	JS161	—	—	—	—
41	*Propter Sion*	—	—	—	—	PW54	—	—
48	*Quod spiritu*	—	GW156	—	—	—	—	—
51a	*Imperator rex Grecorum*	DP	—	—	—	—	—	—
54	*Omne genus*	DP	—	—	HW198	—	—	—

PART II

		DP	GW	JS	HW	PW	OX	co
56	Ianus annum	—	GW162	—	—	—	—	—
59	Ecce chorus	—	—	JS80	hw234	—	—	—
62	Dum Diane	DP	gw30	JS91	hw264	pw30	OX322	—
63	Olim sudor	—	GW36	—	—	—	—	—
66	Acteon, Lampos	DP	—	—	—	—	—	—
69	Estas in exilium	—	—	—	HW272	—	—	—
70	Estatis florigero	DP	—	—	—	—	—	co
71	Axe Phebus	—	GW42	—	—	—	—	—
72	Grates ago	DP	—	—	—	—	—	—
73	Clauso Cronos	—	GW46	—	HW242	—	—	—
74	Letabundus rediit	—	GW172	—	HW214	PW24	—	—
75	Omittamus studia	DP	GW176	JS84	HW202	PW20	—	—
76	Dum caupona	—	GW252	—	—	—	—	—
77	Si linguis	DP	GW50	js105	—	—	ox319	co
78	Anni nove	—	GW170	JS75	HW256	—	—	—
79	Estivali sub fervore	—	—	JS87	—	PW40	—	—
83	Sevit aure	—	GW64	JS112	—	—	—	—
85	Veris dulcis	DP	GW210	JS77	—	—	—	—
86	Non contrecto	—	—	JS117	—	—	—	—
87	Amor tenet	DP	—	JS114	—	—	—	co
88	Amor habet	—	GW166	js118	—	PW26	—	—
88a	Iove cum Mercurio	—	—	—	—	PW34	—	—
90	Exiit diluculo	DP	GW194	JS87	—	—	OX327	—
92	Anni parte	DP	—	js95	—	PW41	—	—
94	Congaudentes ludite	—	—	JS66	—	—	—	—
95	Cur suspectum	DP	—	—	—	—	OX317	—
105	Dum curata	—	—	—	—	PW38	—	—
107	Dira vi amoris	—	—	—	HW258	—	—	—
108	Vacillantes trutine	—	GW178	—	—	—	—	—
111	O comes amoris	DP	GW188	js129	hw254	PW31	OX320	—

		DP	GW	JS	HW	PW	OX	CO
113	*Transit nix*	—	—	—	—	PW28	—	—
114	*Tempus accedit* (= Prata)	DP	—	—	HW250	PW29	—	—
115	*Nobilis, mei*	—	—	—	HW246	—	—	—
116	*Sic mea fata*	DP	GW186	JS120	HW268	—	ox322	—
117	*Lingua mendax*	—	GW182	JS122	—	PW35	—	—
118	*Doleo quod*	DP	—	—	—	—	—	co
119	*Dulce solum*	DP	—	JS130	—	PW23	OX328	—
120	*Rumor letalis*	—	GW68	JS124	—	—	OX328	—
123	*Versa est*	—	GW136	—	—	PW57	—	—
126	*Huc usque*	DP	GW190	JS127	—	PW32	OX330	—
127	*Deus pater*	—	—	JS132	—	PW21	—	—
129	*Exul ego*	DP	GW224	JS50	—	PW19	—	—
130	*Olim lacus*	DP	GW250	JS154	—	—	—	co
131	*Dic Christi*	—	—	—	HW192	—	—	—
135	*Cedit, hiems*	—	GW198	JS68	hw210	—	—	—
136	*Omnia sol*	DP	GW200	JS76	—	PW33	—	CO
137	*Ver redit*	—	GW202	JS63	—	—	—	—
138	*Veris leta*	DP	—	—	—	—	—	co
140	*Terra iam pandit*	—	—	—	HW206	—	—	—
141	*Florent omnes*	—	—	JS89	—	—	—	—
142	*Tempus adest floridum*	—	GW190	—	—	PW25	—	—
143	*Ecce gratum*	DP	—	JS70	—	—	—	CO
144	*Iamiam virent*	—	GW204	JS69	HW212	—	—	—
145	*Musa venit*	—	GW196	js79	HW238	—	—	CO
145a	*Were diu werlt* (= Vvere div)	DP	—	—	—	—	—	CO
148	*Floret tellus*	DP	—	—	—	—	OX318	—
149	*Floret silva*	DP	—	—	—	—	—	CO
151	*Virent prata*	—	—	JS82	—	—	—	—
156	*Salve, ver*	—	GW206	JS72	HW232	—	—	—
157	*Lucis orto*	DP	—	—	—	PW39	OX324	—
158	*Vere dulci*	DP	GW214	js86	—	—	OX326	—
160	*Dum estas*	—	GW212	JS74	HW262	—	—	—
161	*Ab estatis*	—	—	—	HW218	—	—	—
162	*O consocii*	—	—	JS142	—	—	—	—
167	*Laboris remedium*	—	GW216	—	—	—	—	—
167a	*Swaz hie gat umbe*	DP	—	—	—	—	—	CO

169	Hebet sidus	—	GW72	—	—	—	—	—
171	De pollicito	—	—	JS78	—	—	—	—
174	Veni, veni	DP	—	JS107	—	—	—	CO
177	Stetit puella	DP	gw220	—	—	—	ox327	co
178	Volo virum	DP	—	—	HW228	PW36	—	—
179	Tempus est iocundum	DP	GW218	JS64	HW222	—	—	co
180	O mi dilectissima	DP	—	—	—	—	—	co
183	Si puer	DP	—	JS111	—	—	—	CO
185	Ich was ein chint	DP	—	—	—	—	—	—
186	Suscipe, Flos	DP	—	JS106	HW252	—	—	—

PART III

191	Estuans intrinsecus	DP	GW106	JS55	hw170	PW14	ox263	co
193	Denudata veritate	DP	GW238	JS144	—	—	—	—
195	Si quis Deciorum	—	GW262	—	—	—	—	—
196	In taberna	DP	GW226	js135	—	PW18	—	CO
197	Dum domus	DP	—	—	—	—	—	—
200	Bacche, bene	—	GW230	—	—	—	—	—
202	O potores exquisiti	—	GW234	JS151	HW184	—	—	—
206	Hircus, quando	—	GW280	—	—	—	—	—
207	Tessera, blandita	DP	—	—	—	—	—	—
210	Qui cupit egregium	DP	—	—	—	—	—	—
211	Alte clamat Epicurus	—	GW248	—	—	—	—	—
216	Tempus hoc letitie	DP	GW222	—	—	—	—	—
219	Cum 'In orbem'	DP	GW272	JS42	—	PW11	—	—
222	Ego sum abbas	DP	—	JS158	—	—	—	CO

SUPPLEMENT

s2*	Ich lob	DP	—	—	—	—	—	—	—
s3*	Iam dudum estivalia	DP	—	—	—	—	—	—	—
s16*	Chramer, gip	dp	—	—	—	—	—	—	co

Index of First Lines

Original lines (Latin or Middle High German) are printed in italics, English translation in Roman.

An equals sign indicates that the line listed is not the first line of the piece from which it comes, or is a variant reading of it.

A few pieces have recognized titles: these are also listed, and are indicated by inverted commas.

Strict alphabetical order is followed, word spaces being ignored.